UNOFFICIAL
TAYLOR SWIFT
FRIENDSHIP BRACELETS

33 Bead Designs Through the Eras

DOVER PUBLICATIONS
Garden City, New York

Many words and phrases used in this book are words from albums and songs by
Taylor Swift® and may be trademarks registered by TAS Rights Management,
including, without limitation, the following:
1989,® Blank Space,™ folklore,™ Look What You Made Me Do,® Lover,™ . . . Ready for It?,®
Reputation,® Swiftie,® Swifties,® Taylor Swift,® Taylor's Version,™
and The Tortured Poets Department.™

Unofficial Taylor Swift Friendship Bracelets: 33 Bead Designs Through the Eras is a new work,
first published by Dover Publications in 2025.
This book is unofficial and unauthorized. It is not licensed, approved, or endorsed by
Taylor Swift,® Taylor Swift® Productions Inc., Universal Music Group, or any affiliated associates.

ISBN-13: 978-0-486-85433-5
ISBN-10: 0-486-85433-7

Publisher: Betina Cochran
Acquisitions Editors: Allyson D'Antonio and Shannon Lawlor
Managing Editorial Supervisor: Susan Rattiner
Senior Production Editor: Michael Croland
Cover Designer: Peter Donahue
Creative Manager and Interior Designer: Marie Zaczkiewicz
Production: Pam Weston, Tammi McKenna, Ayse Yilmaz

Printed in China
85433701   2025
www.doverpublications.com

CONTENTS

THE BRACELETS

CONTENTS

CONTENTS

WHAT ARE THE ERAS?

Taylor Swift® fans, or Swifties,® are one of the most connected and dedicated fan bases in the world. Swifties® bond over everything related to Taylor, from her heart-wrenching lyrical bridges to her iconic looks. So when Taylor announced The Eras Tour in November 2022, fans rushed to the internet to express their excitement. The concept of the tour was fascinating. Taylor would hold her fans' hands and walk them through her eras. Revisiting old eras might seem like a new concept, but the eras have been a theme Taylor has leaned into throughout her career. She reinvents her look with each new album to match its aesthetic. New eras bring exciting new albums, new looks, and incredible themes for the corresponding tour. Taylor's creativity has kept fans searching for "Easter eggs" that hint at what her next move—and era—will be.

The Eras Tour gave longtime fans a chance to revisit their favorite eras of Taylor's career. It gave her new audience the opportunity to experience older music live. It gave Taylor the opportunity to promote the albums she rerecorded so that she could own her music.

INTRODUCTION

When fans were brainstorming ways to dress up for Taylor's tour, they took inspiration from a song on her new album, *Midnights*. In "You're on Your Own, Kid," Taylor sings, "Make the friendship bracelets/Take the moment and taste it." This line inspired fans to make friendship bracelets for The Eras Tour. This evolved into a bonding activity among Swifties.® Trading bracelets at the show quickly became a trend. Young girls and boys arrived at shows with their arms covered in colorful friendship bracelets. They were ready to trade these bracelets with newfound friends.

Taylor's music not only connects her to her fans but also connects her fans to each other. The friendship bracelets have become a physical embodiment of the camaraderie, connection, and friendship that Taylor's music has brought into every fan's life. This connection should be embraced and celebrated. Now, let's learn how to make our own Swiftie® friendship bracelets to trade!

MATERIALS

❤ Stretch® Magic Bead & Jewelry Cord (0.5 mm diameter) or similar elastic cord

❤ Bead needles

❤ 4 mm seed beads in a variety of colors and finishes

❤ A–Z letter beads

❤ Scissors

❤ B7000 Clear Glue with Precision Tips

❤ Painter's tape or Scotch® Magic™ Tape

OPTIONAL MATERIALS

❤ Symbol beads

❤ Tweezers

❤ Measuring tape

INSTRUCTIONS

For the 33 bead patterns in this book, your bracelet will have a diameter of approximately 2.5 inches. To make the bracelet bigger or smaller, increase or decrease the pattern.

❤ Take the cord, and cut between 7 and 9 inches—or longer, depending on the width of your wrist.

> **TIP:** If you don't have measuring tape, cut a length that's roughly equal to the length of two-thirds of your forearm.

❤ Gently stretch the cord by pulling and wrapping it around your hands. This will reduce the chances of the bracelet snapping and provide more cord to work with.

❤ Fold a piece of painter's tape or Scotch® Magic™ Tape over the end of the cord. This will prevent the beads from falling off.

❤ Place the end of the cord that isn't taped through the eye of a beading needle. Slowly add the beads on the cord.

INSTRUCTIONS (CONTINUED)

- After finishing a pattern to the desired length, gather both ends of the cord. Tie them tightly.

> **TIP:** To make the knot more secure, use a fisherman's knot.

- Cut off the tape. Then weave the loose ends of the cord under the beads to either side of the knot. Trim off the excess.

- Add a small drop of B7000 glue to the knot to prevent it from unraveling. Allow 24 hours for the bracelet to dry.

TAYLOR SWIFT
FRIENDSHIP BRACELETS

TAYLOR SWIFT® (DEBUT)
Era

- ❤ Original Release Date: October 24, 2006

- ❤ Years: 2006–08

- ❤ Popular Songs: "Teardrops on My Guitar," "Our Song," "Should've Said No"

- ❤ Themes: Young love, longing, teenage heartbreak

- ❤ Symbols: Curly hair, glittery guitar, little black dress

- ❤ Summary: Taylor's self-titled debut album marked her entry into the country music world. Immediately, she captured the hearts of young girls across the globe. Her debut album was composed while she was still in high school. The themes of heartbreak, love, and longing reflect the emotions and experiences many of her fans were having.

Taylor's debut introduced the world to a future icon.
It claimed her spot as America's next rising star.

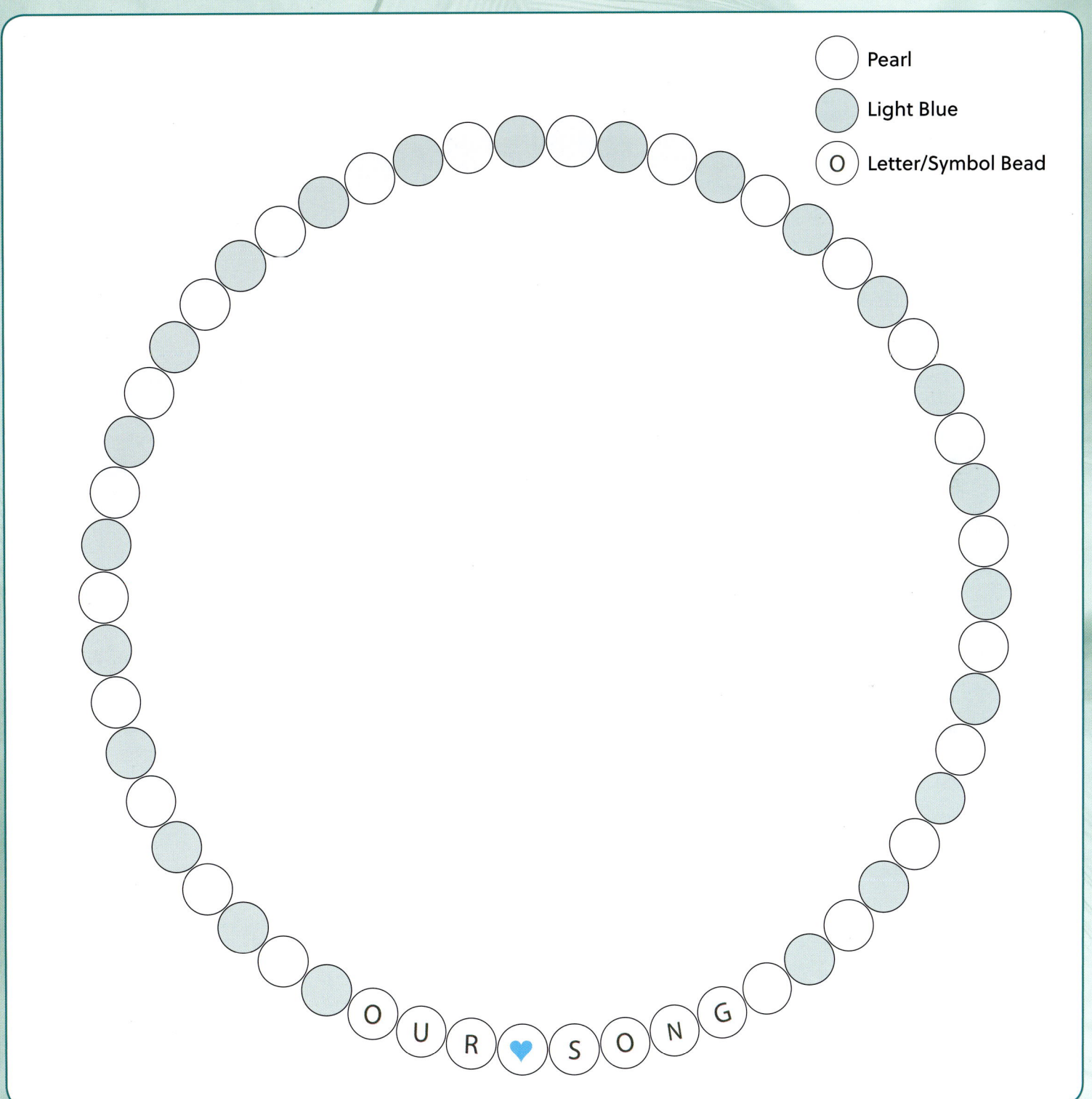

Pearl

Light Blue

O Letter/Symbol Bead

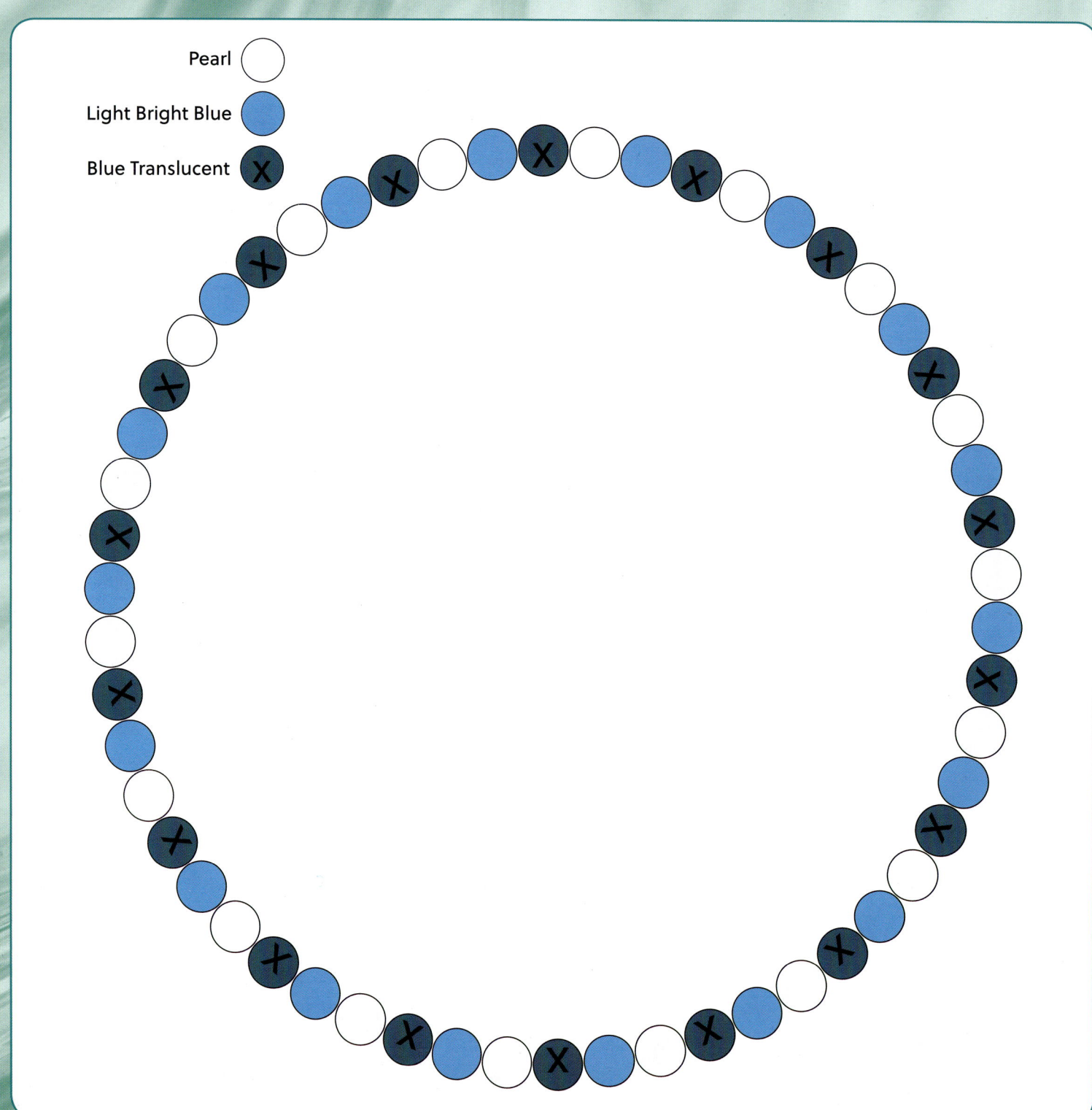

Pearl

Light Bright Blue

Blue Translucent

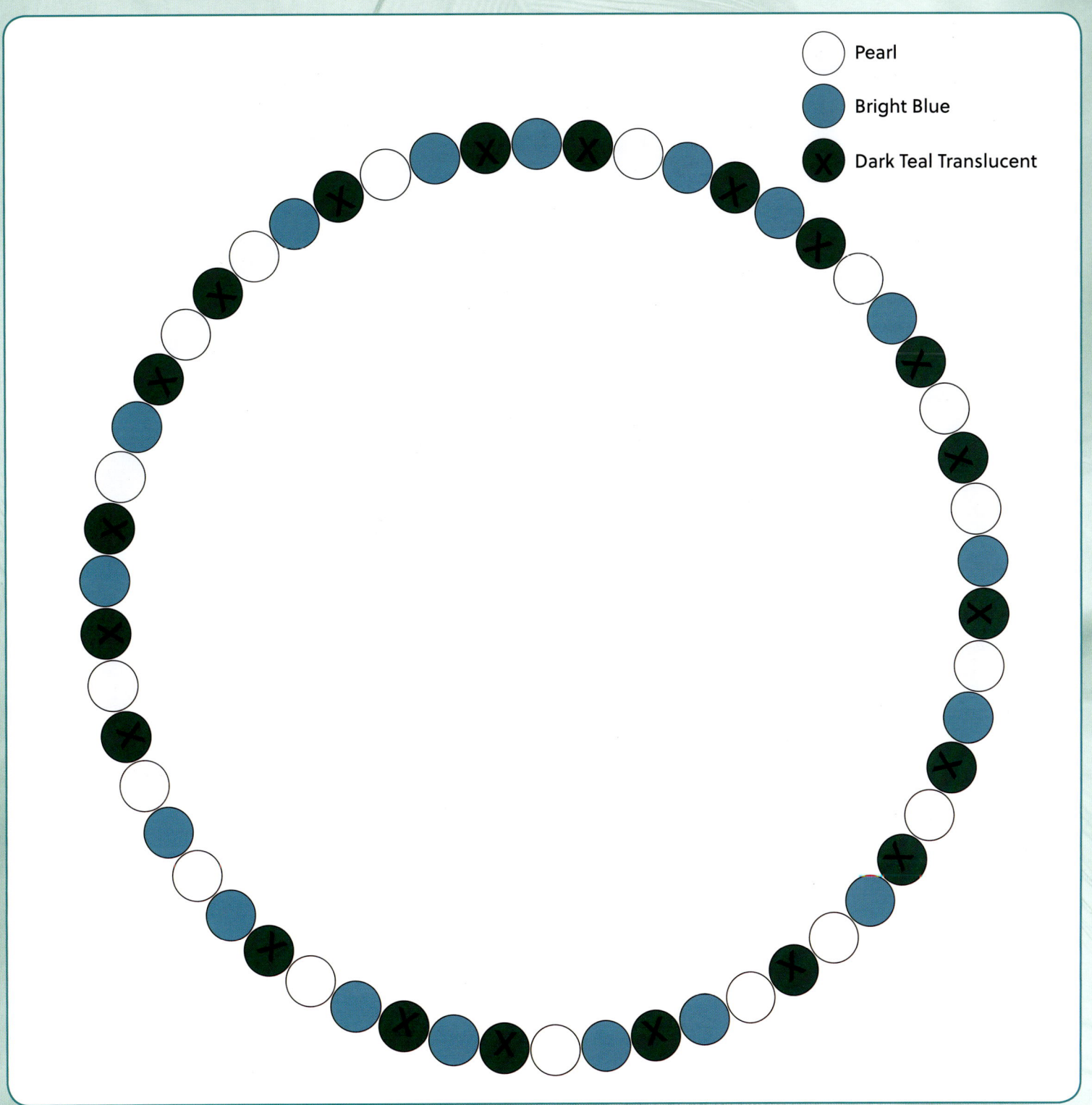

Pearl

Bright Blue

Dark Teal Translucent

FEARLESS
Era

❤ Release Date: November 11, 2008
Taylor's Version™ Release Date: April 9, 2021

❤ Years: 2008–10

❤ Popular Songs: "You Belong with Me,"
"Love Story," "Fifteen"

❤ Themes: Young love, fairy tales, innocence, nostalgia

❤ Symbols: The number 13, sparkly dresses, hand hearts

❤ Summary: Taylor followed her debut with a magical album that focused on the feelings that come with being an innocent teenager first finding their place in the world. *Fearless* encapsulated the beauty of young love, being a teenager, and learning how to navigate friendships.

Taylor fearlessly tackled the fairy-tale feelings
that blossom with young love.

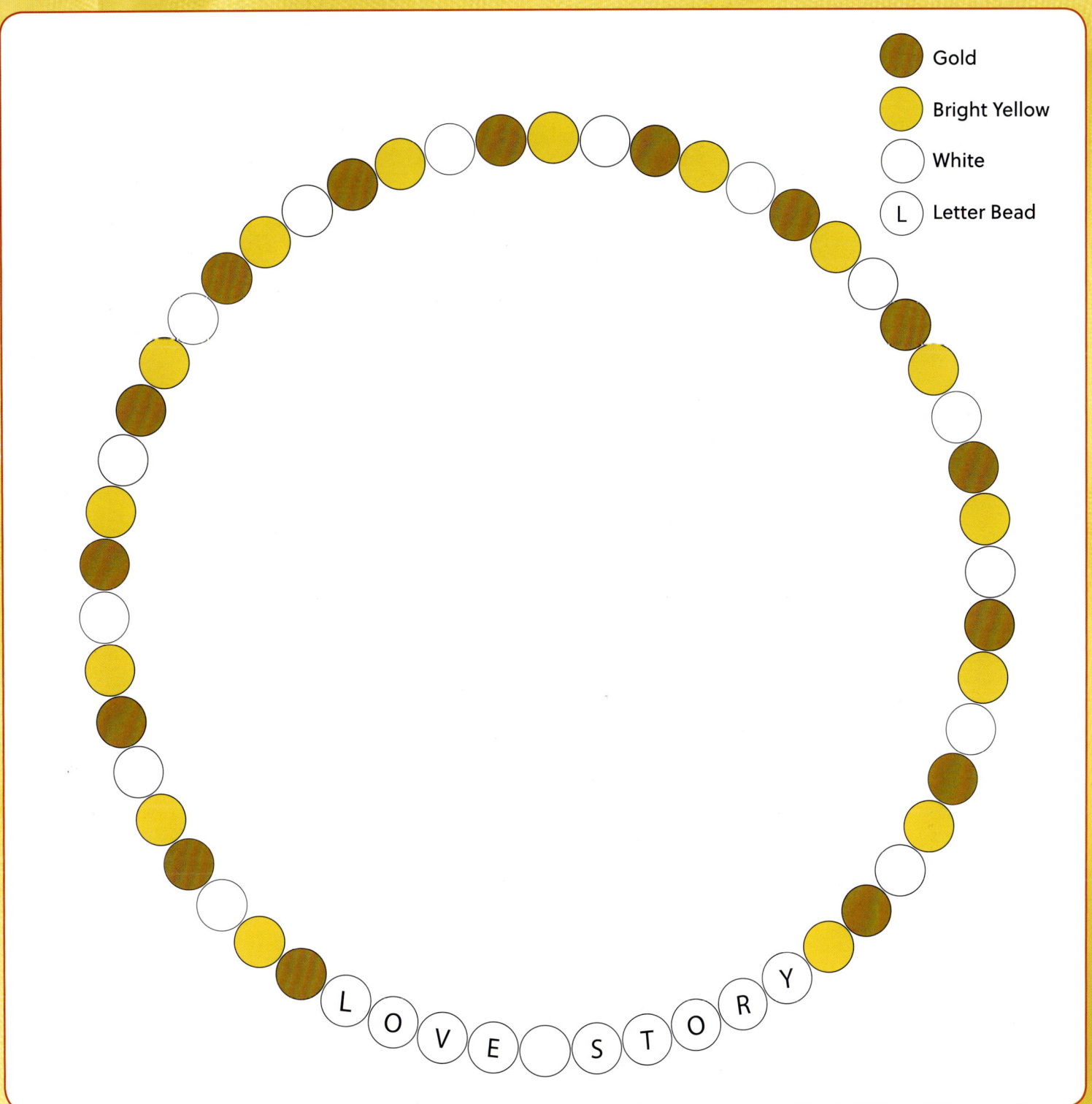

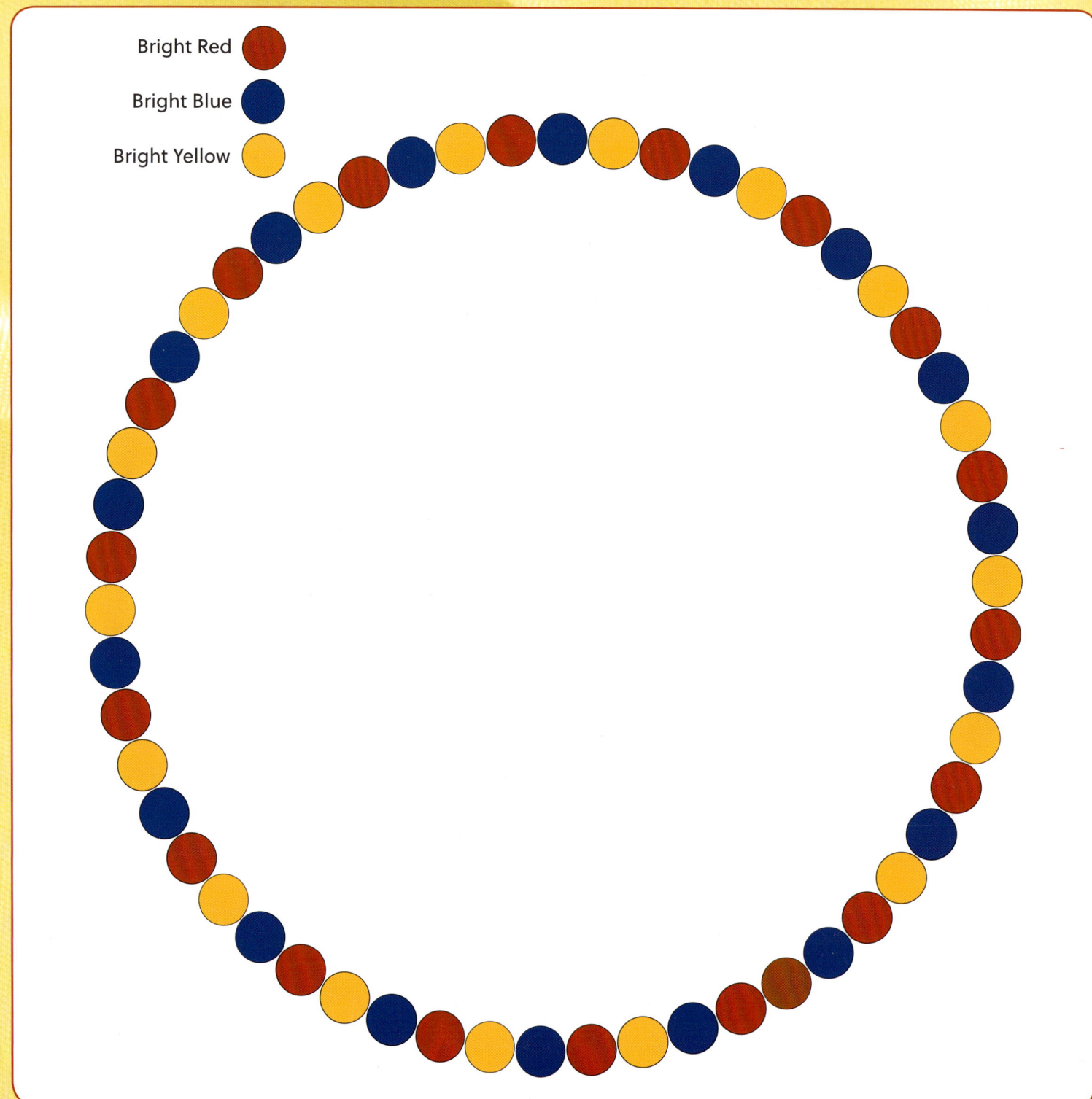

Bright Red

Bright Blue

Bright Yellow

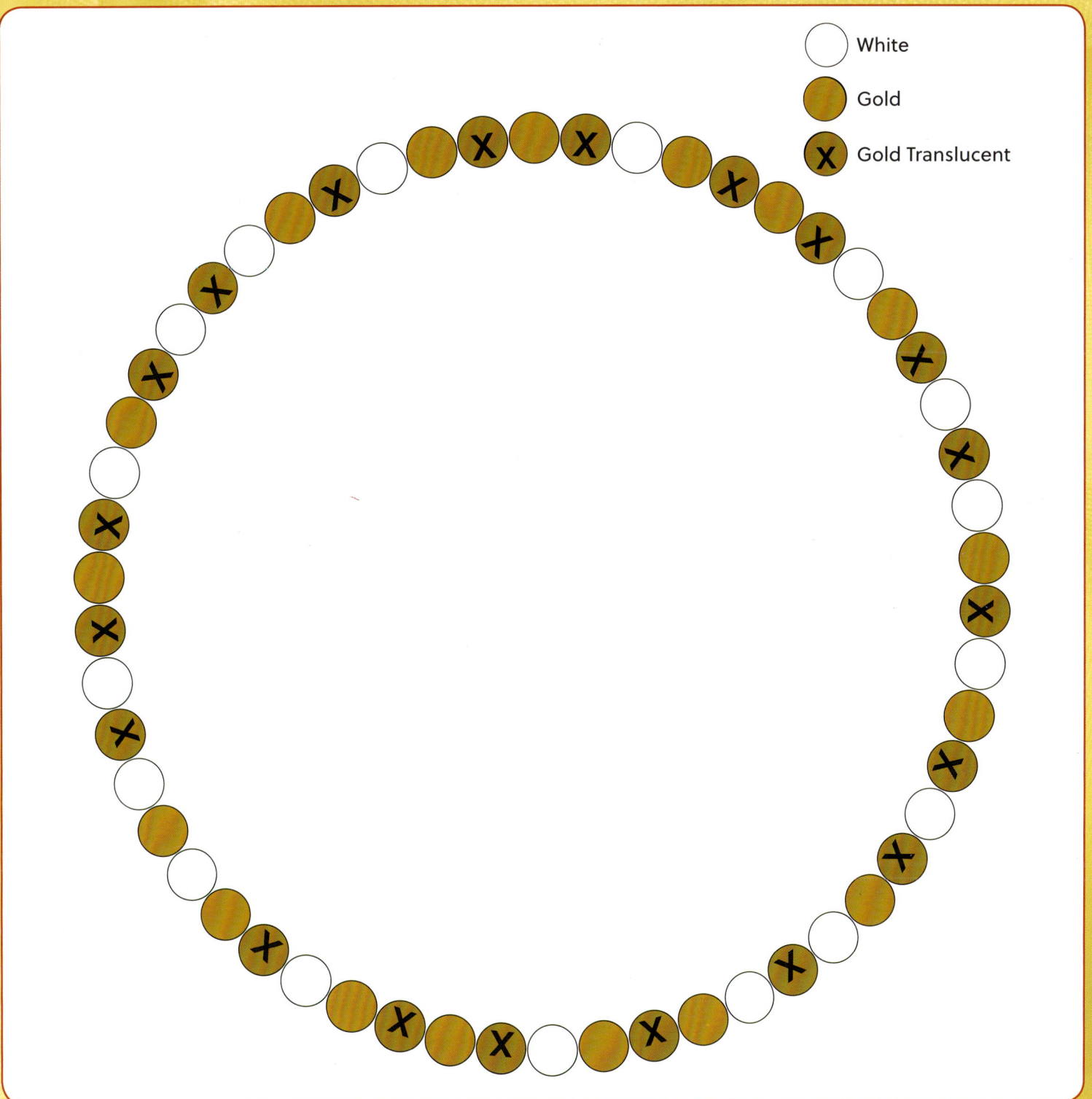

SPEAK NOW
Era

- ♥ Release Date: October 25, 2010
  Taylor's Version™ Release Date: July 7, 2023

- ♥ Years: 2010–12

- ♥ Popular Songs: "Mine," "Enchanted," "Back to December," "Dear John"

- ♥ Themes: Acceptance, falling in love, dealing with hate, breakups

- ♥ Symbols: Purple dress, fireworks, ball gowns

- ♥ Summary: *Speak Now* was Taylor's third album. It focused on themes surrounding love, heartbreak, dealing with hate, and learning how to speak your mind. This era included a lot of extravagant dresses, purple outfits, and bold confrontations—through song—with her critics.

Speak Now encouraged young listeners to always speak their truth.

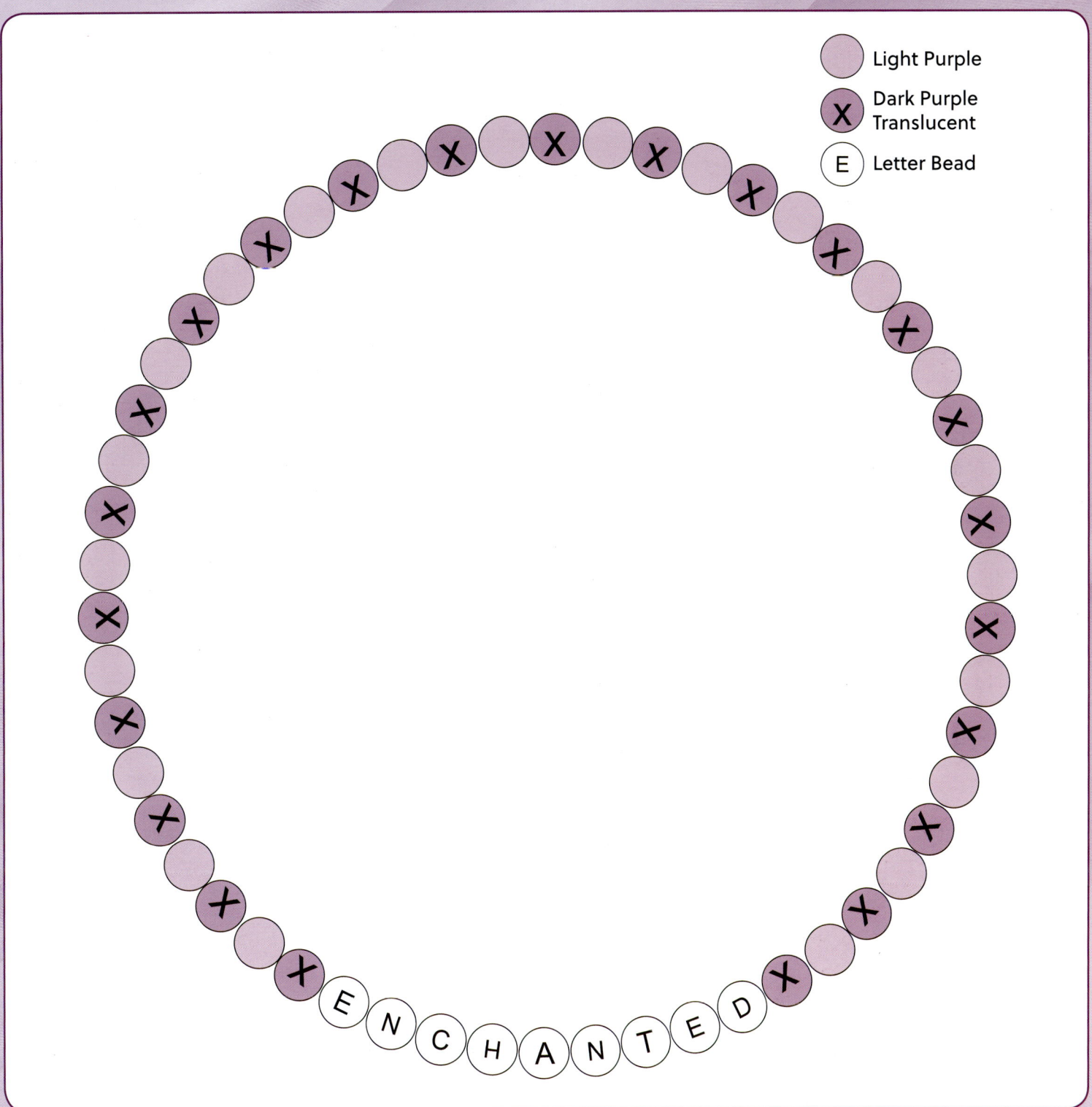

Light Purple

X Dark Purple Translucent

E Letter Bead

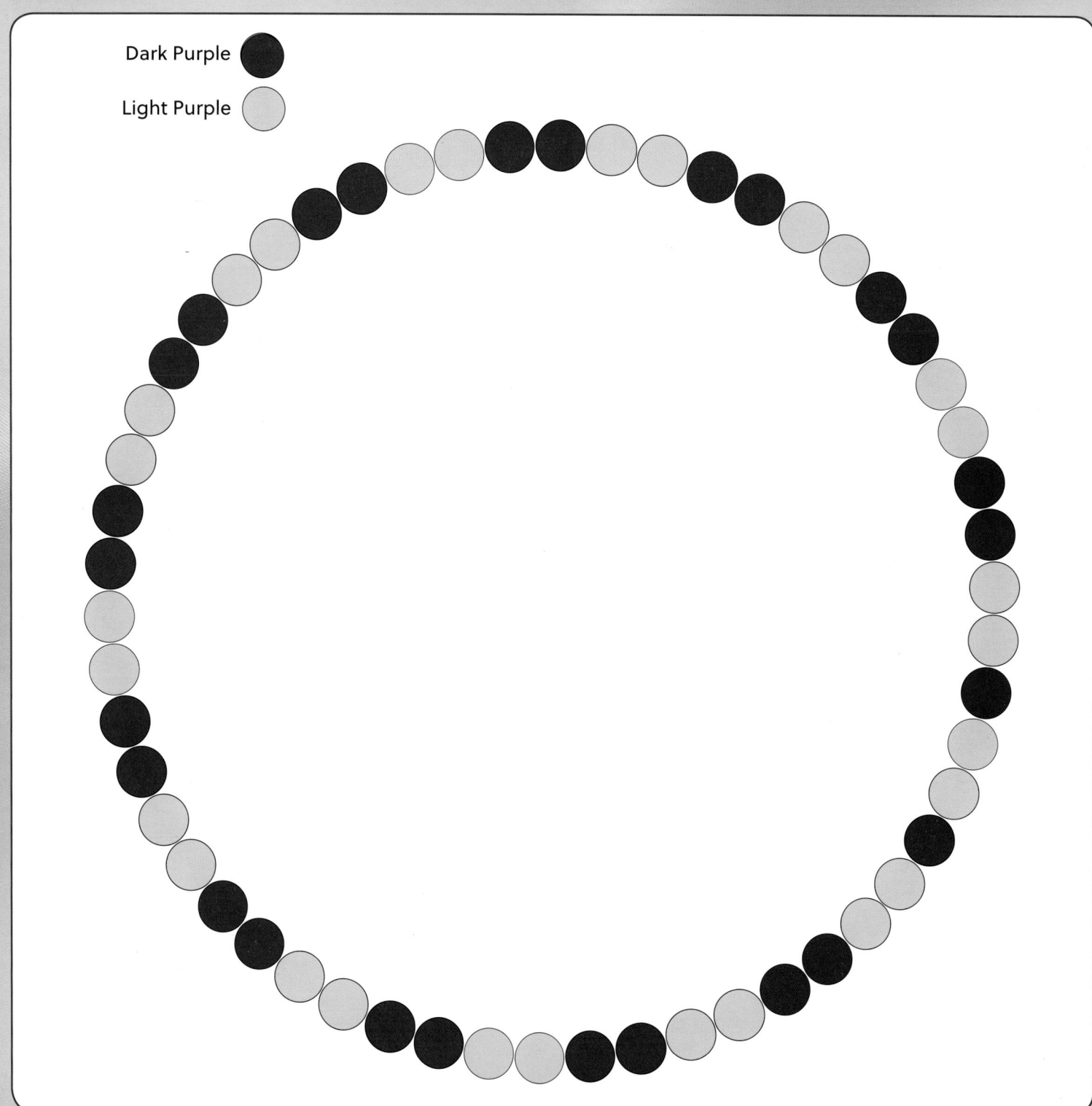

Dark Purple

Light Purple

Dark Purple

Bright Pink/Purple

X Purple Translucent

RED
Era

❤ Release Date: October 22, 2012
Taylor's Version™ Release Date: November 12, 2021

❤ Years: 2012–14

❤ Popular Songs: "I Knew You Were Trouble,"
"Red," "We Are Never Ever Getting Back Together,"
"All Too Well (10 Minute Version)" [from *Red (Taylor's Version)*™]

❤ Themes: Heartbreak, empowerment, healing

❤ Symbols: Red lipstick, red scarf

❤ Summary: Taylor's fourth album, *Red*, introduced listeners to her vibrant Red Era. The album painted a vivid picture of deep heartbreak. It took listeners on a roller coaster of intense emotions—hence the bright, intense color the album was named after. *Red* is a breakup album that is also about letting go and moving on from the loss of a relationship. The songs describe what it feels like to grieve and reflect on heartache.

Red was about letting go and moving on from heartbreak . . .
while wearing gorgeous red lipstick.

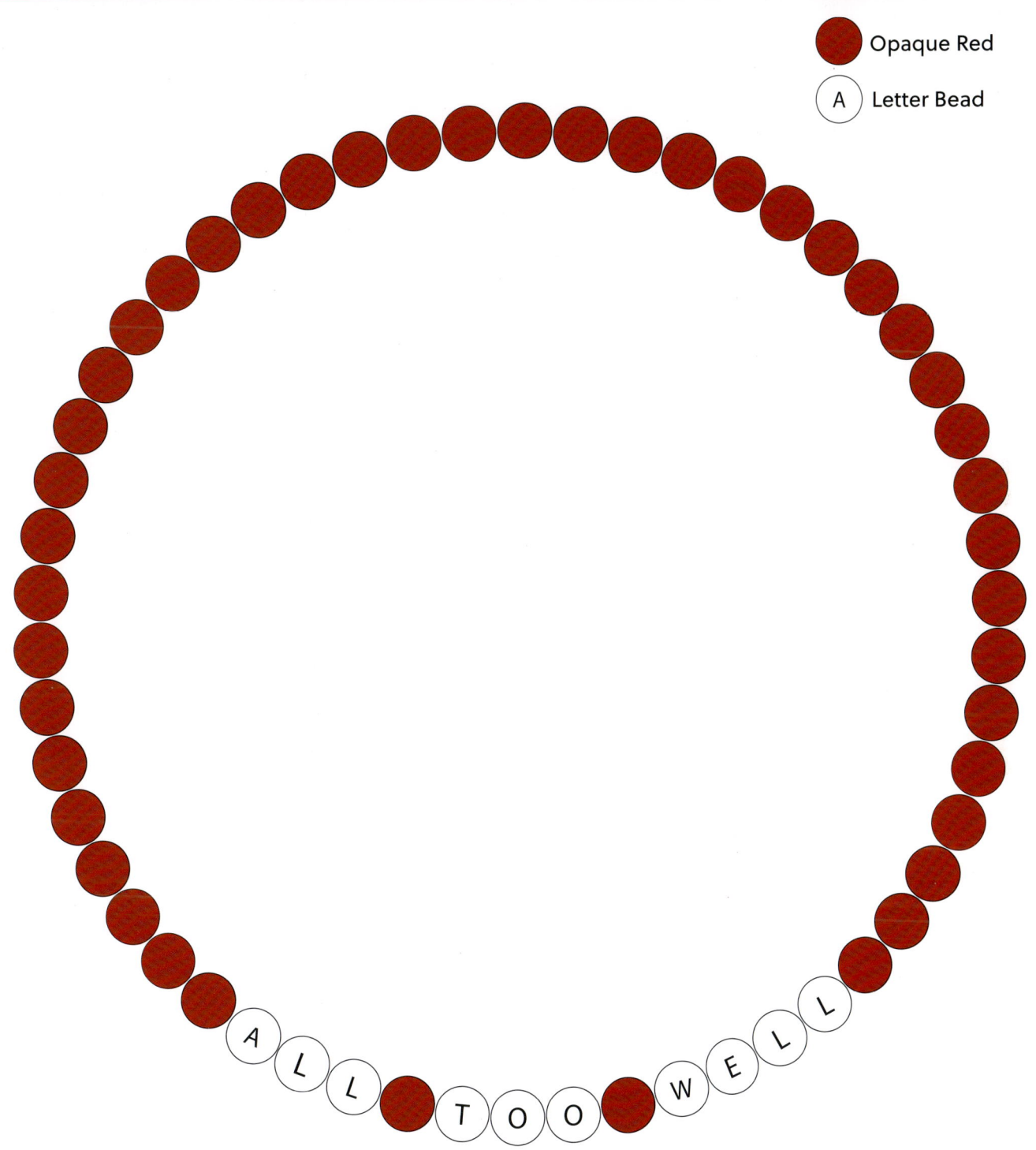

Opaque Red

A Letter Bead

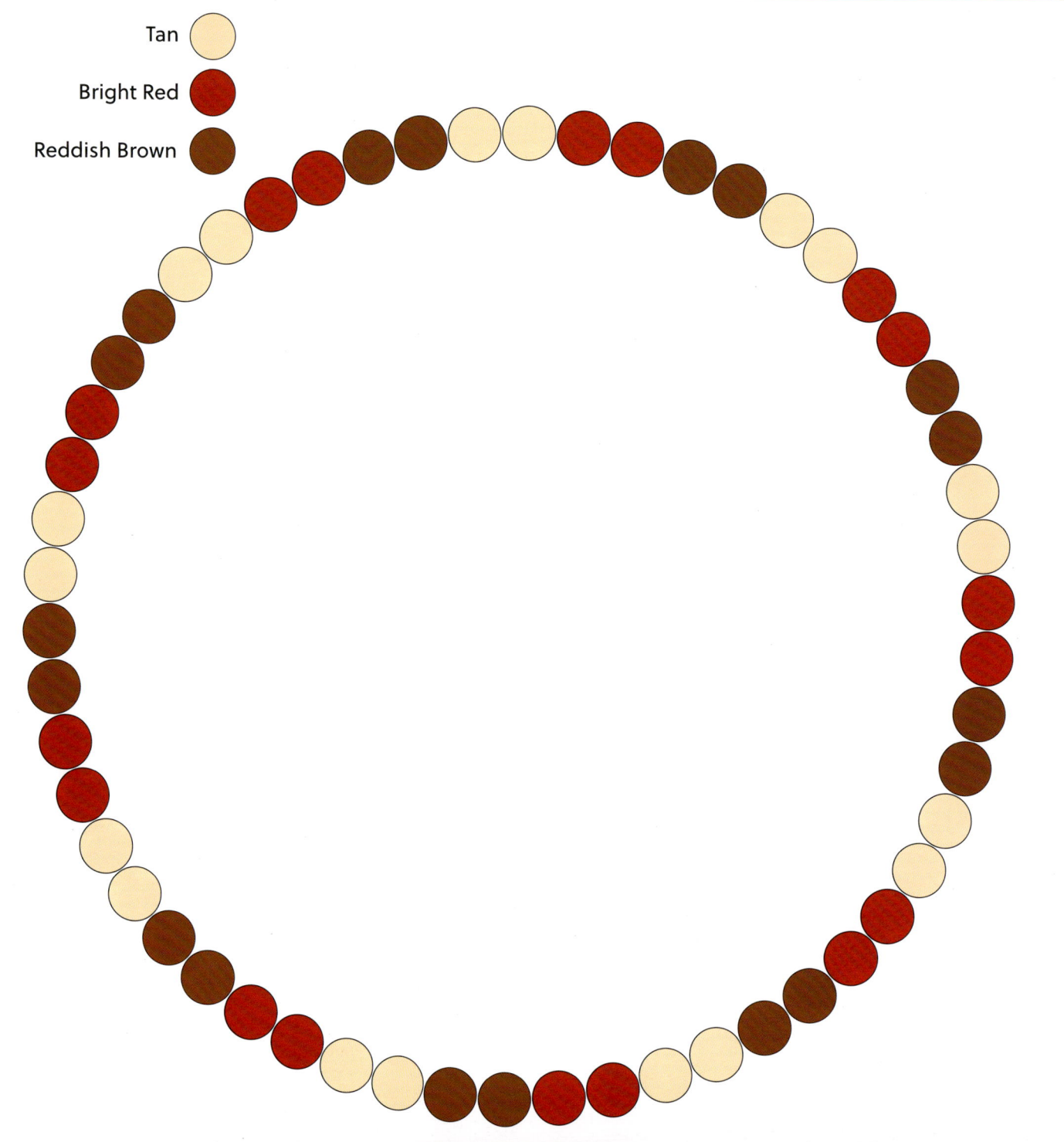

Tan

Bright Red

Reddish Brown

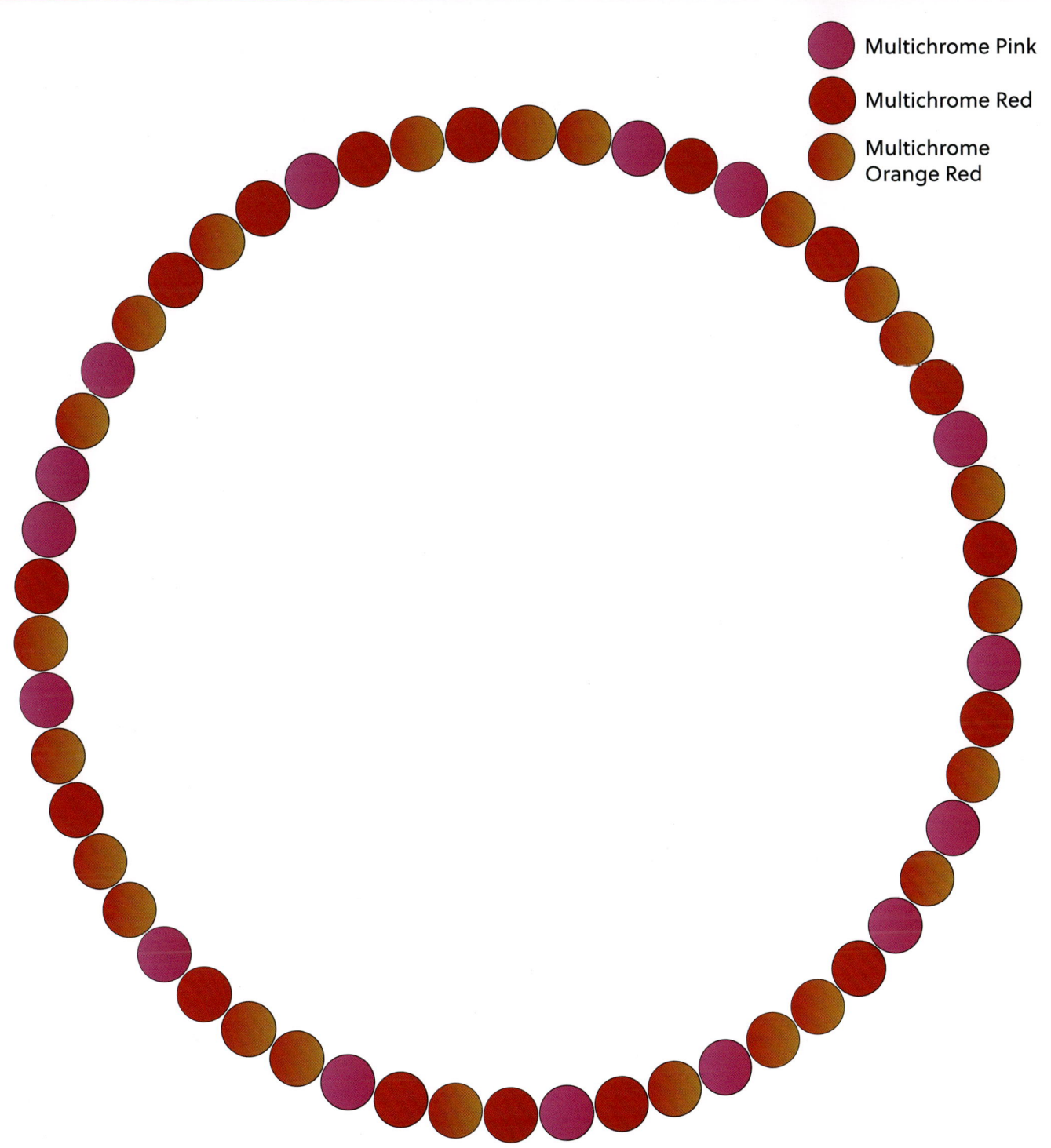

Multichrome Pink

Multichrome Red

Multichrome Orange Red

1989®

Era

- 💙 Release Date: October 27, 2014
  Taylor's Version™ Release Date: October 27, 2023

- 💙 Years: 2014–17

- 💙 Popular Songs: "Shake It Off," "Style,"
  "Blank Space,"™ "Welcome to New York"

- 💙 Themes: Friendship, moving to New York, love

- 💙 Symbols: New York City, seagulls, beach

- 💙 Summary: Taylor's switch from country to pop was solidified with the release of *1989*®. Her fifth album, which was named after her birth year, follows Taylor as she begins her time in New York. Her *1989*® era focused on typical experiences many young adults have, such as heartbreak, going out with friends, and experiencing a new city.

1989® brings listeners on Taylor's journey to NYC as she experiences new heartbreaks and relationships, and focuses on herself and her friends.

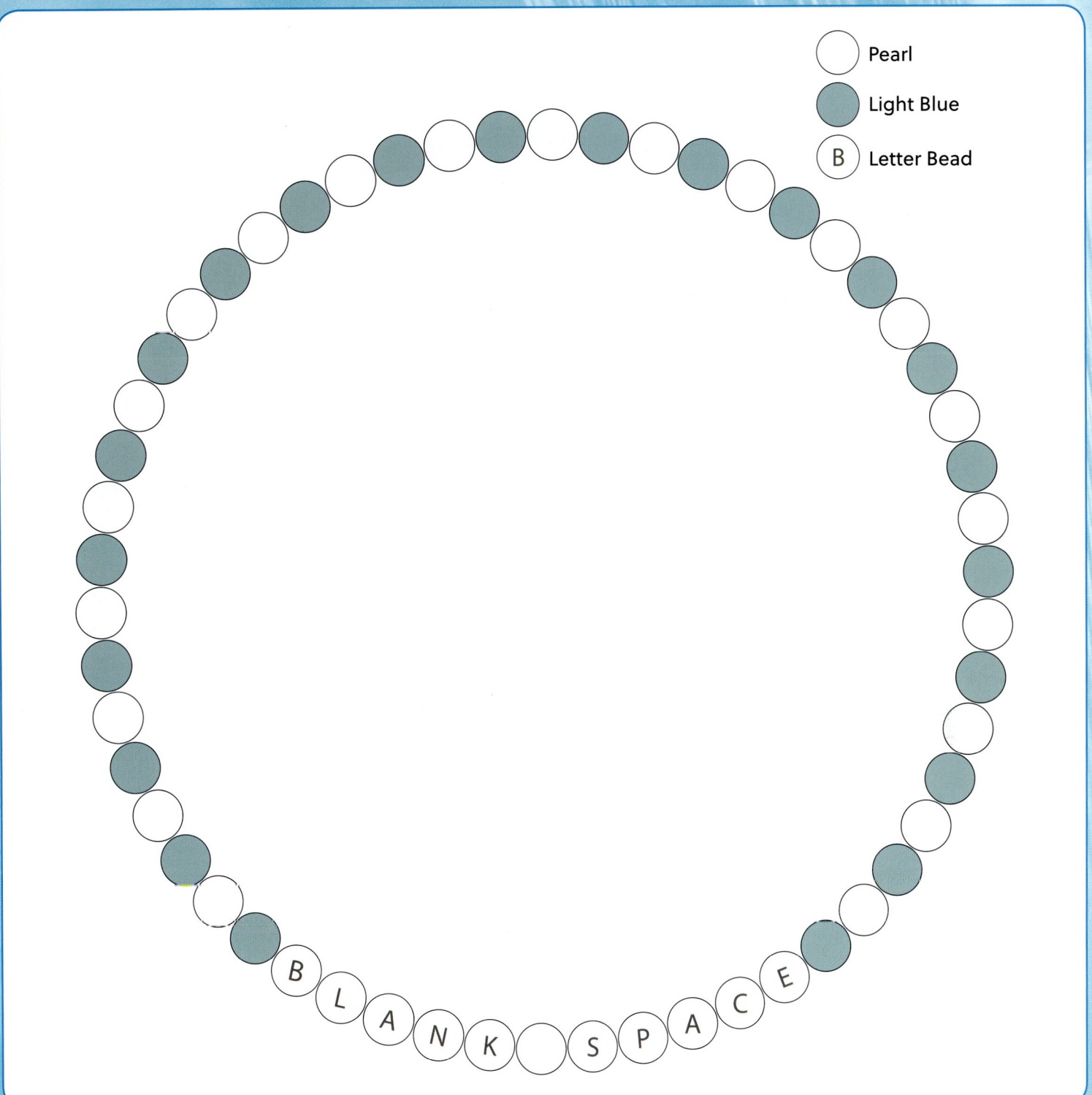

Pearl

Light Blue

B Letter Bead

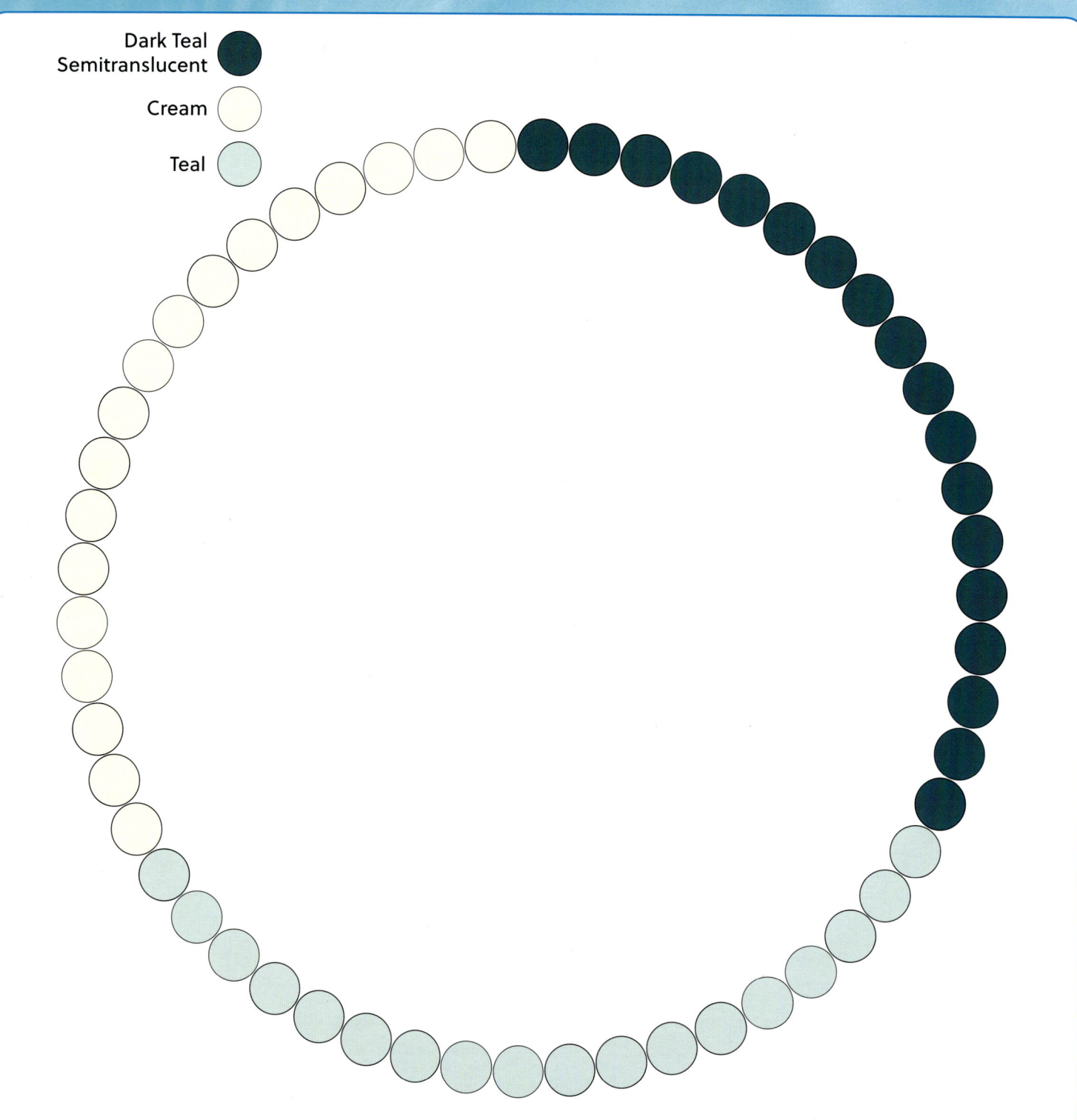

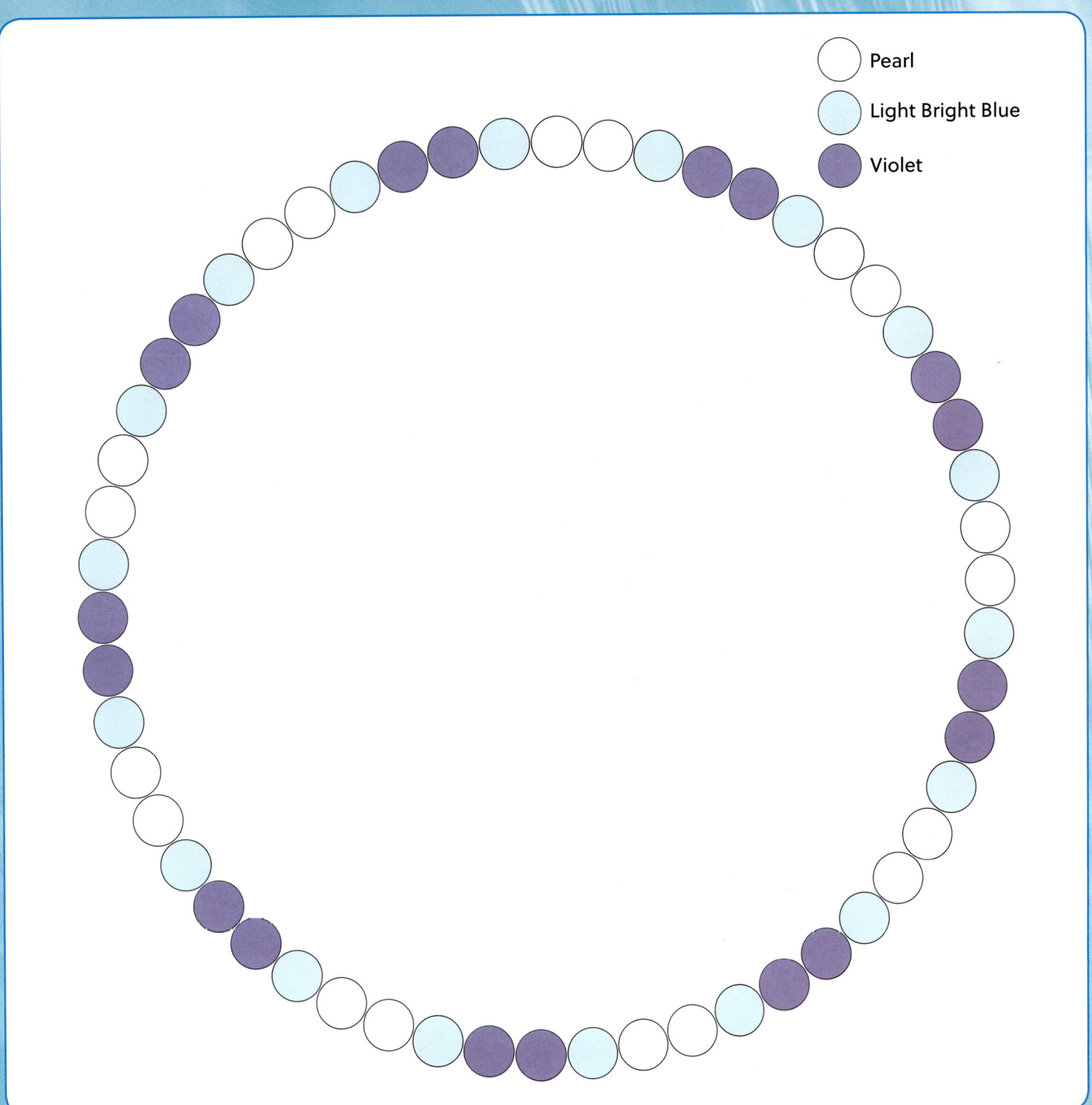

Pearl

Light Bright Blue

Violet

REPUTATION®
Era

- ♥ Release Date: November 10, 2017

- ♥ Years: 2017–19

- ♥ Popular Songs: "Look What You Made Me Do,"® "Call It What You Want," "Delicate," ". . . Ready for It?"®

- ♥ Themes: Revenge, private love, anger

- ♥ Symbols: Snakes, tombstones, black leotards, jewels

- ♥ Summary: Taylor went into hiding for a year after the public turned against her. In her year away from the media, Taylor found a private love that inspired several songs on *Reputation*.® Her sixth album was a response to the public hate and drama. This era was a major comeback for Taylor following a public celebrity feud.

The bold and unapologetic attitude of *Reputation*®
was all about reclaiming your image.

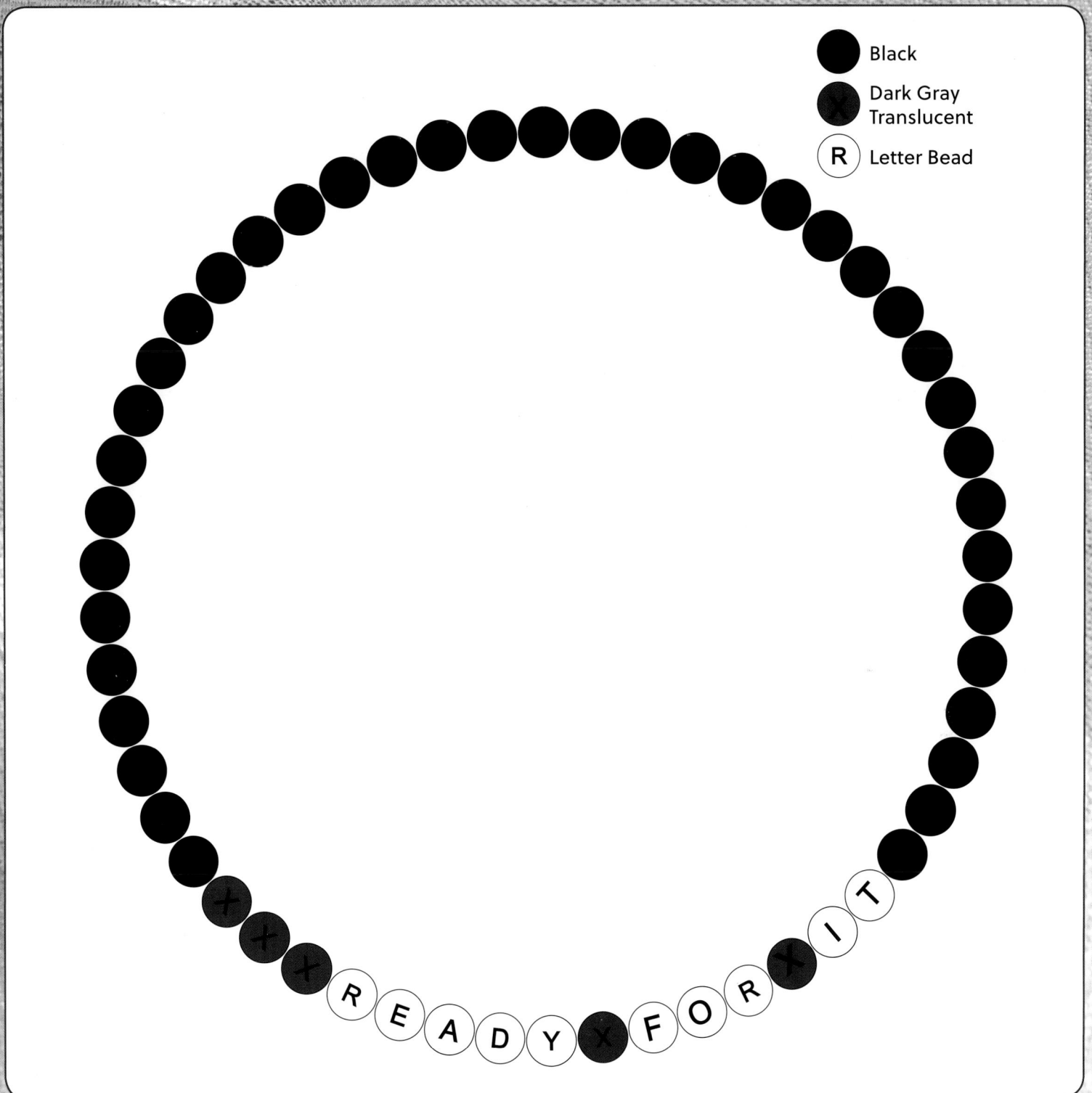

Black

Dark Gray Translucent

Letter Bead

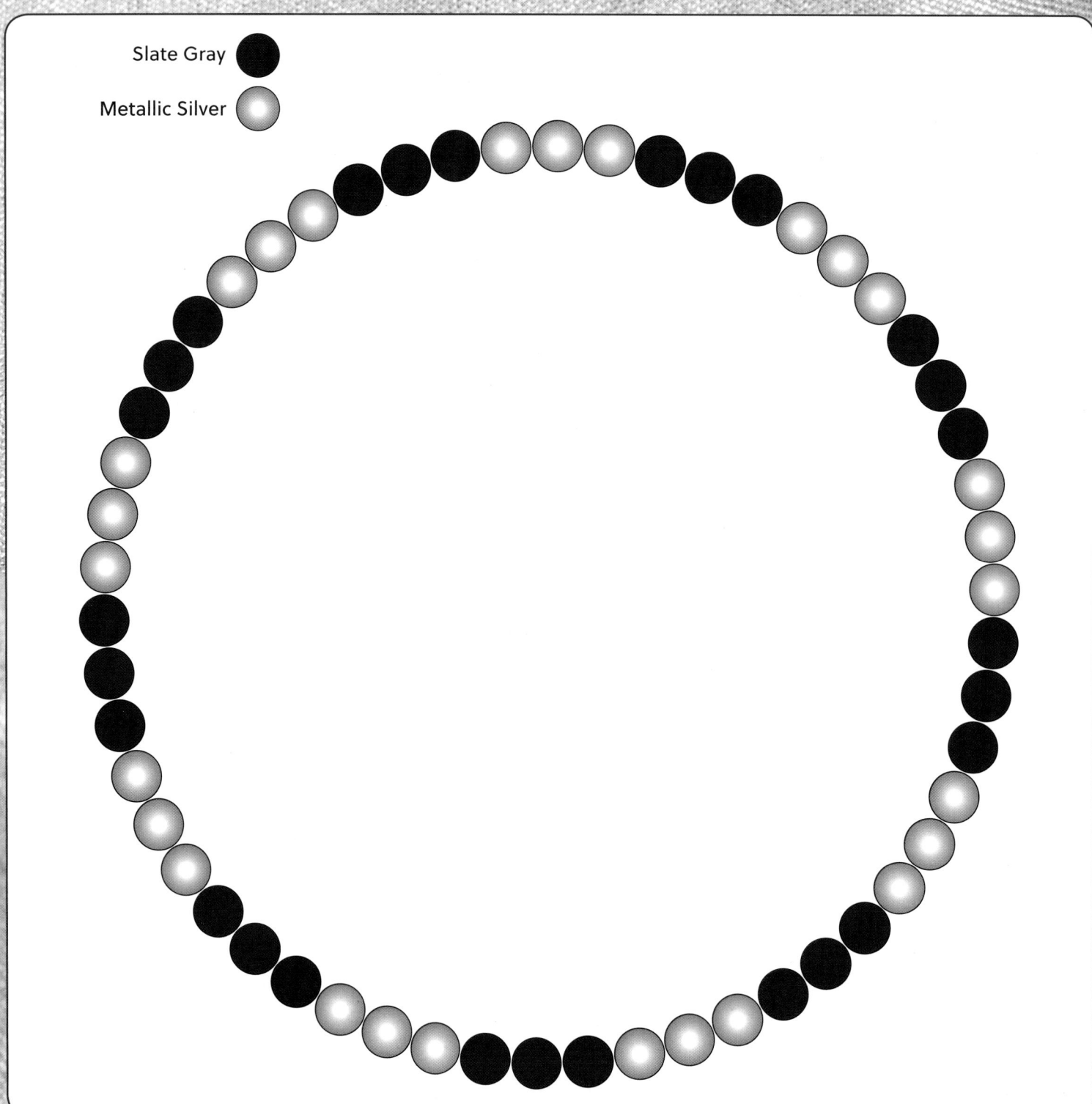

Slate Gray

Metallic Silver

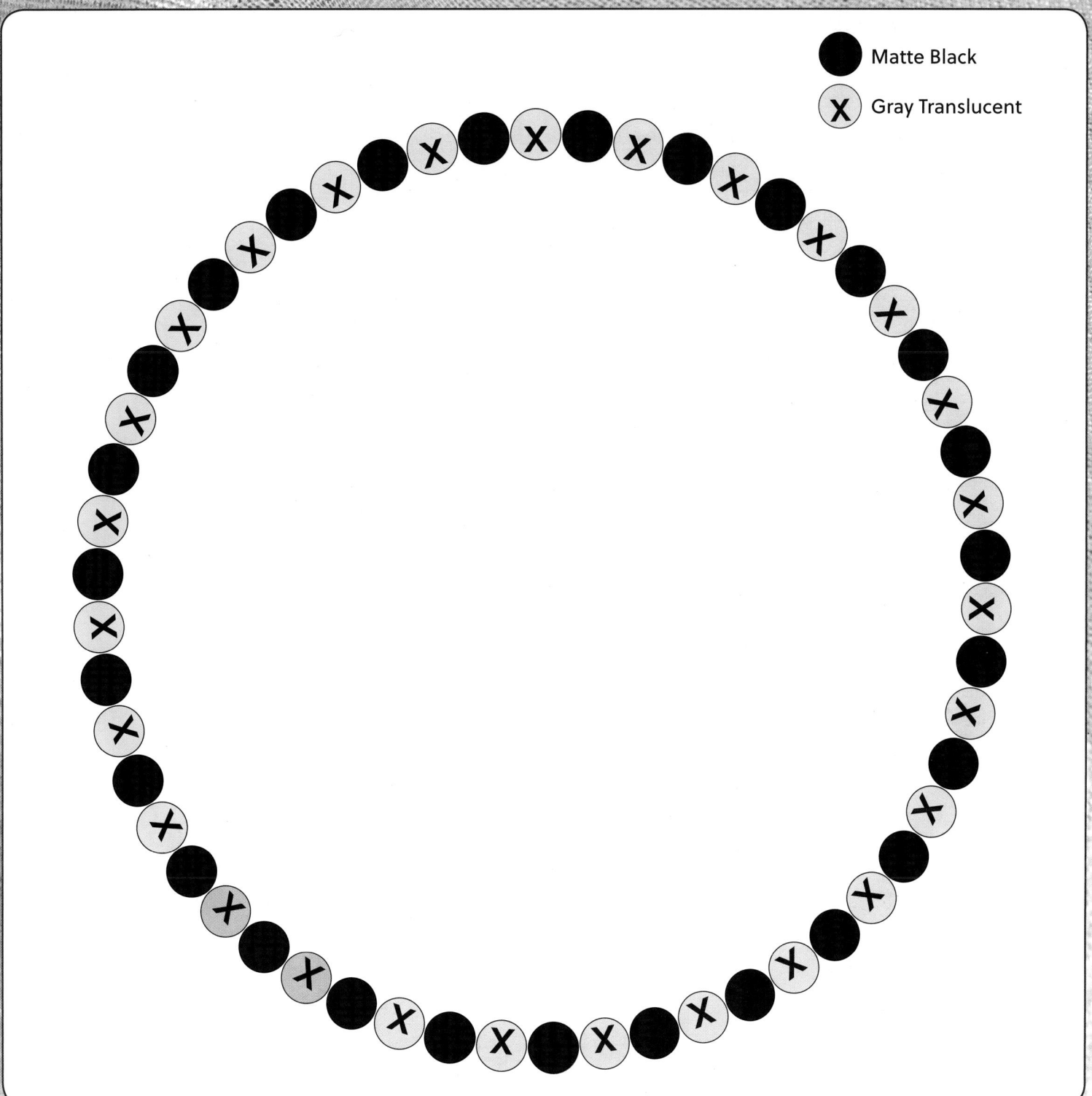

Matte Black

Gray Translucent

LOVER™
Era

💚 Release Date: August 23, 2019

💚 Years: 2019–20

💚 Popular Songs: "Cruel Summer,"
"Cornelia Street," "You Need to Calm Down"

💚 Themes: Falling in love, committed love,
anxiety, loneliness

💚 Symbols: Sunrise, pink pastels, flowers

💚 Summary: *Lover*™ was Taylor's seventh album. This colorful era was a love note to her romantic life. She explored the feelings of falling in love, the fear of losing love, and the anxiety of overthinking in a relationship. Taylor canceled her *Lover*™ tour because of the COVID-19 pandemic.

The *Lover*™ era embraced all the complicated
and messy feelings that go along with falling in love.

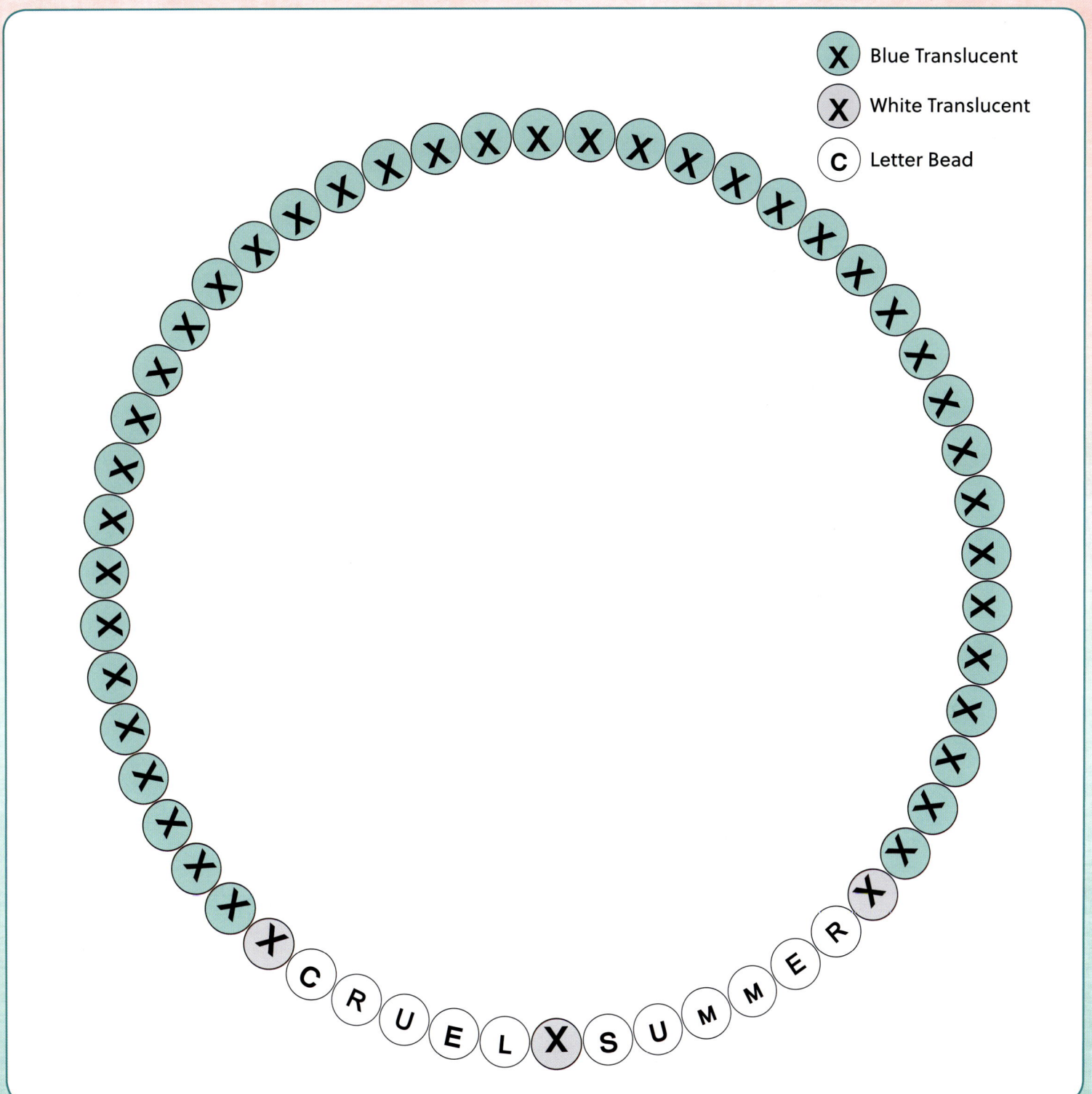

X Blue Translucent

X White Translucent

C Letter Bead

CRUEL X SUMMER

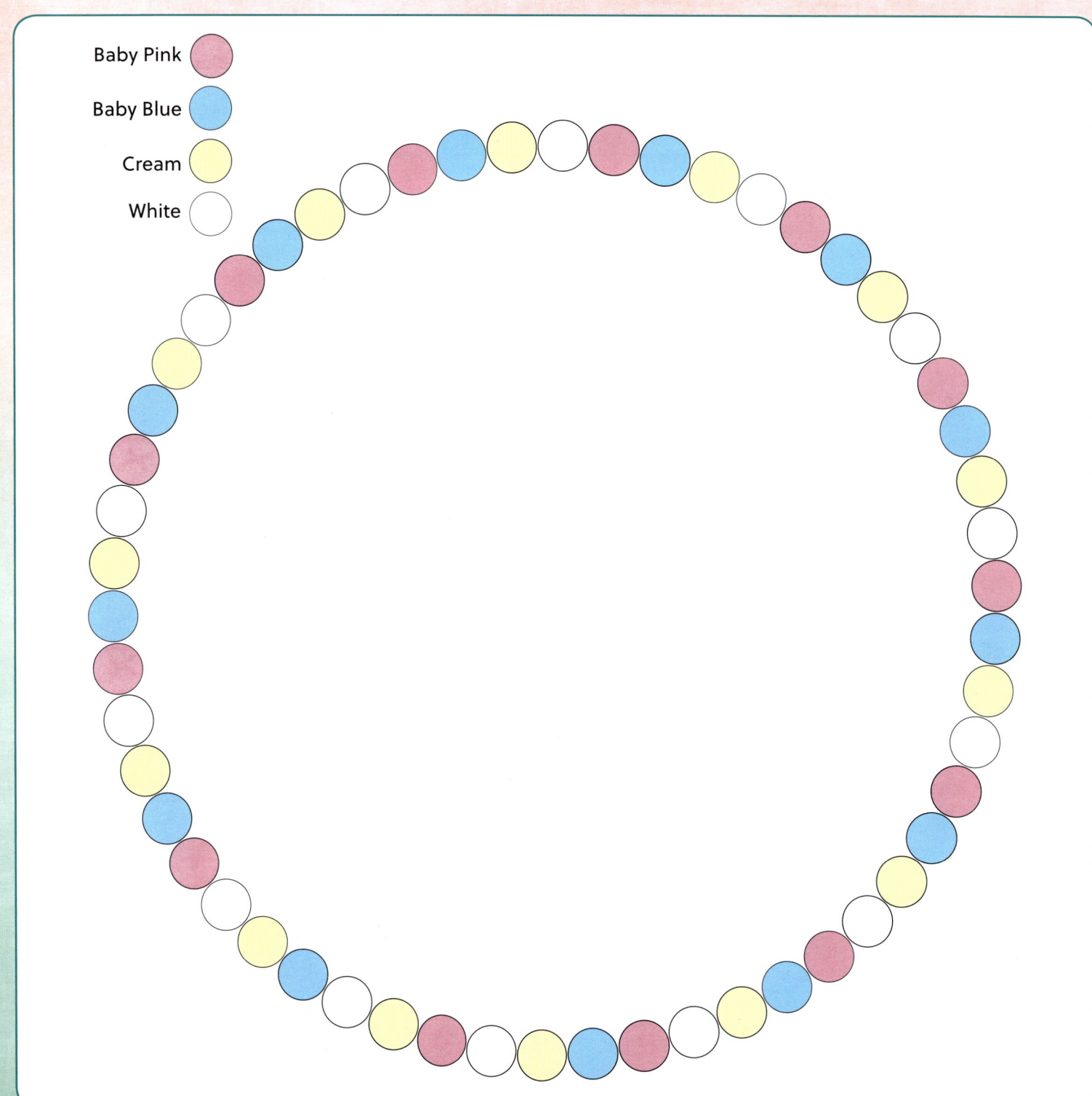

Baby Pink

Baby Blue

Cream

White

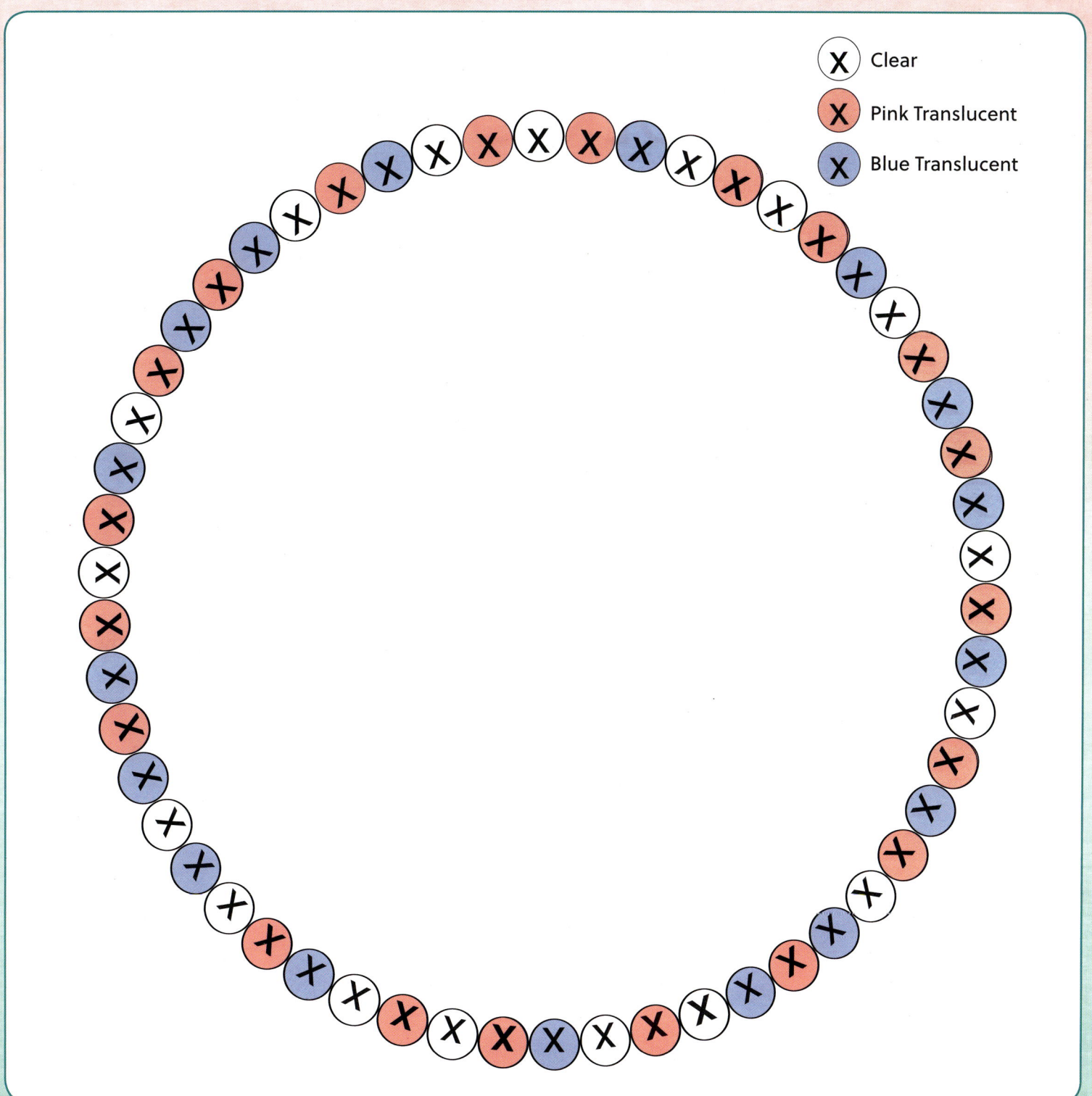

X Clear

X Pink Translucent

X Blue Translucent

FOLKLORE™
Era

- Release Date: July 24, 2020

- Years: 2020–22

- Popular Songs: "august," "betty," "cardigan"

- Themes: Heartbreak, love, relationship dynamics

- Symbols: Woods, grassy piano, magic

- Summary: Taylor's eighth album, *folklore*,™ was released during the COVID-19 lockdown. Taylor created an alluring collection of characters. She followed each of their stories to explore various relationship dynamics and drama. Fans loved the narrative twist to the lyrics.

Fans fell in love with the characters on *folklore*.™
Many people saw pieces of themselves woven
in throughout the narrative.

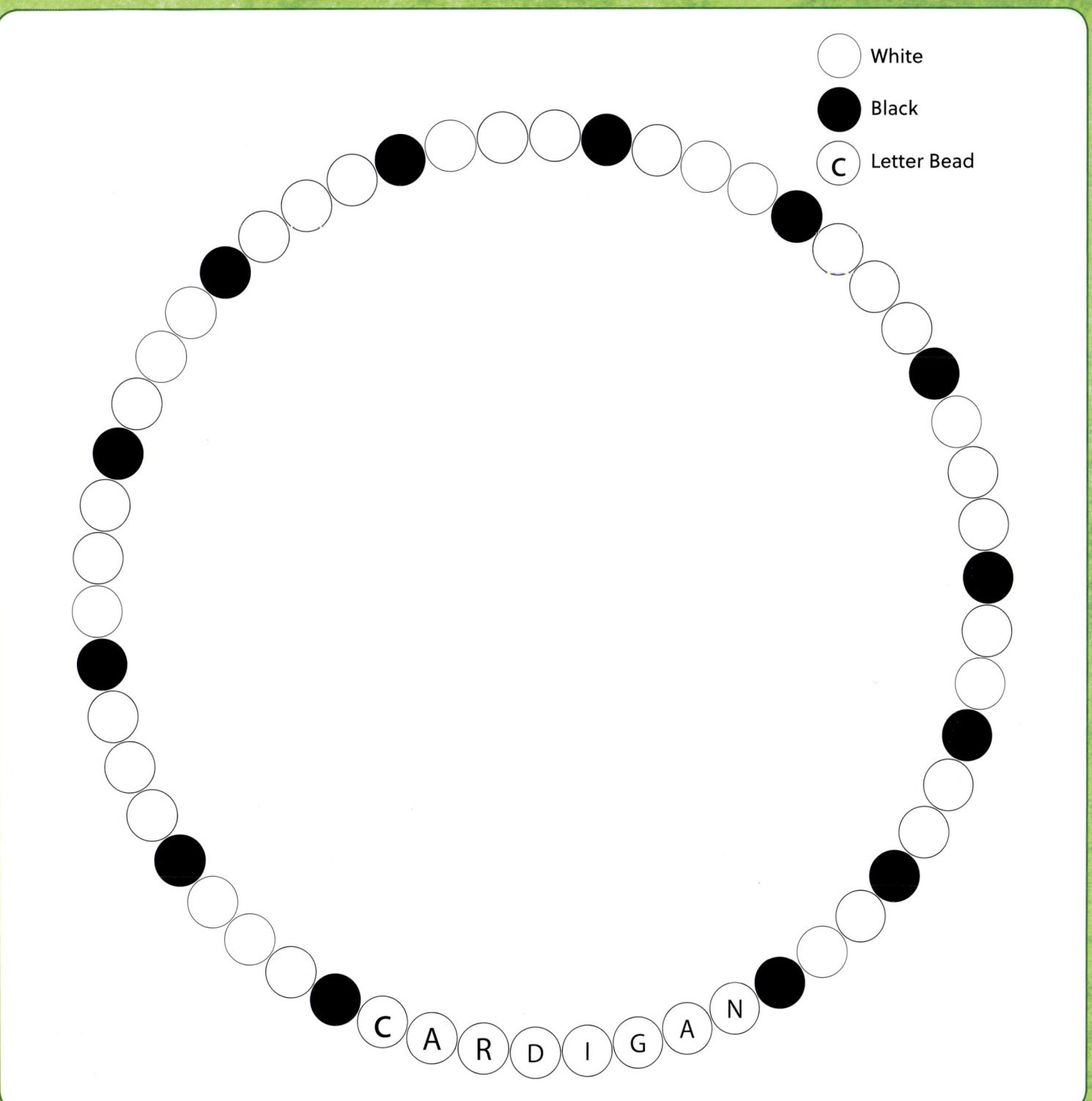

White

Black

C Letter Bead

Dark Gray Translucent X

Beige Translucent X

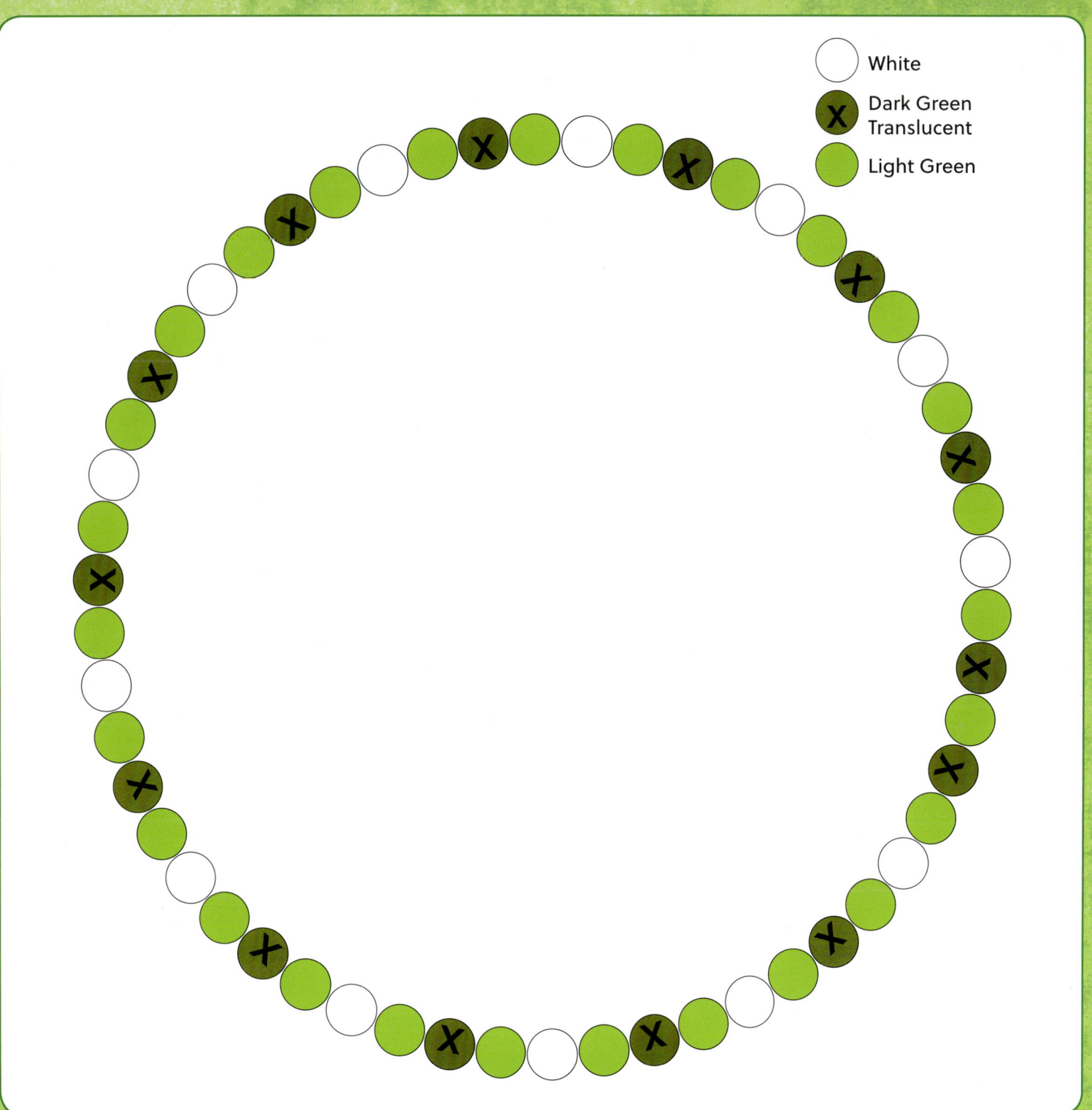

White

Dark Green Translucent

Light Green

EVERMORE
Era

- ❤ Release Date: December 11, 2020

- ❤ Years: 2020–22

- ❤ Popular Songs: "champagne problems," "willow," "tolerate it," "no body, no crime"

- ❤ Themes: Heartbreak, love, relationship dynamics

- ❤ Symbols: Willow trees, snow, winter cape

- ❤ Summary: Taylor's ninth album, *evermore*, was closely tied to *folklore*.™ Taylor surprised her fans with this sister album to *folklore*.™ *evermore* had similar aesthetics, but with a winter twist.

evermore dove deeper into the narrative
Taylor weaved with *folklore*,™ exploring the stories of characters
every fan could relate to.

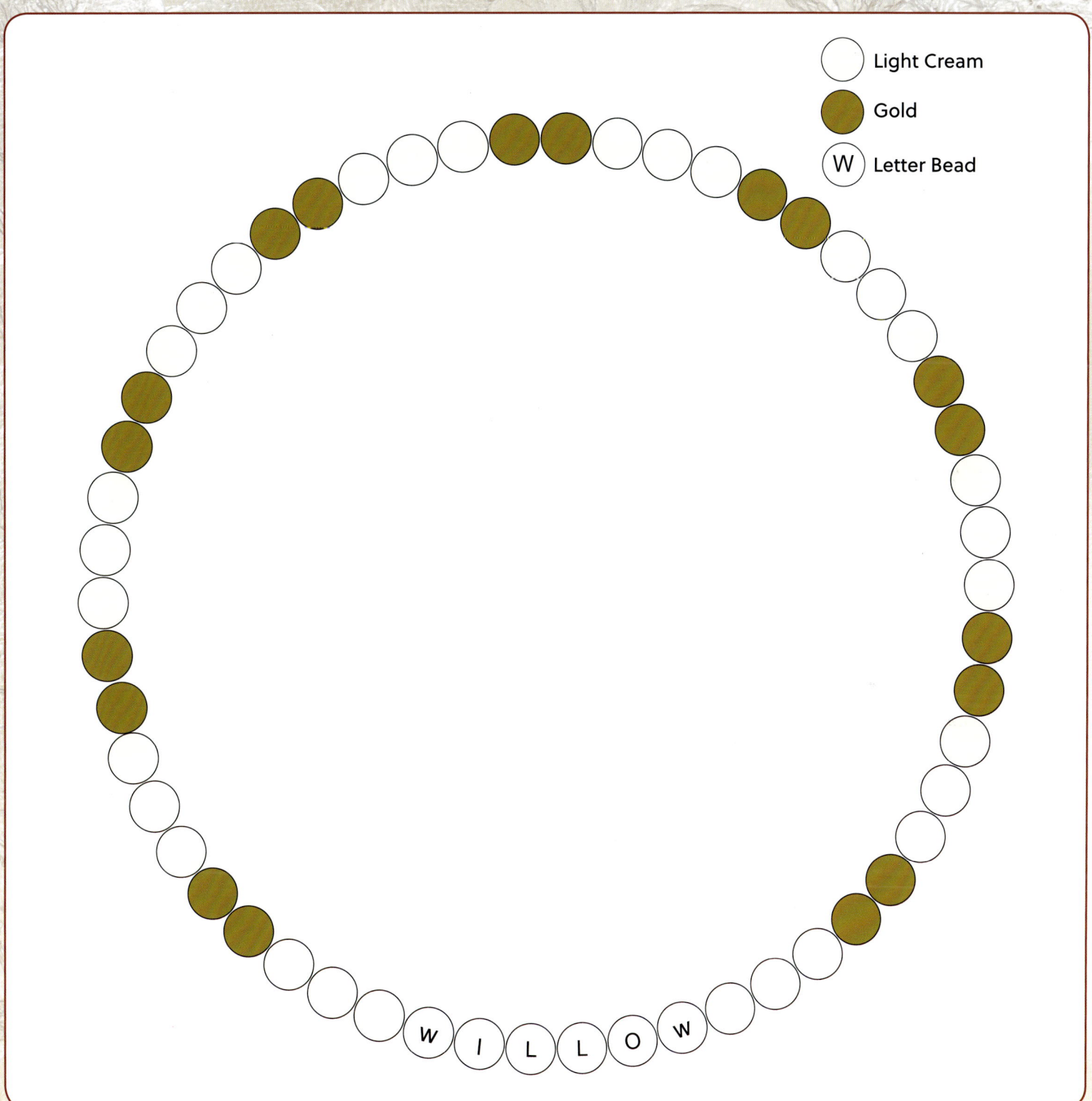

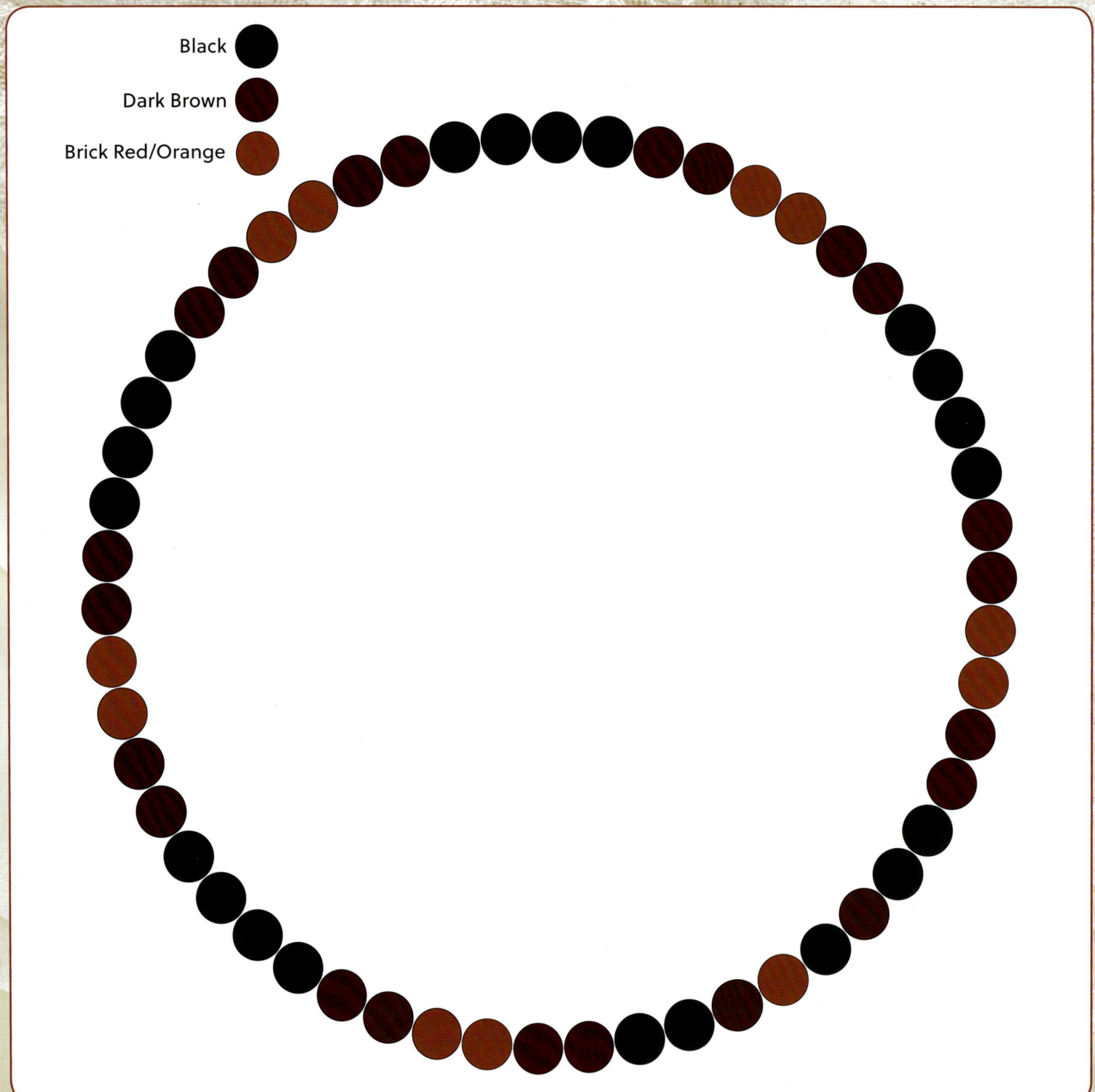

Black

Dark Brown

Brick Red/Orange

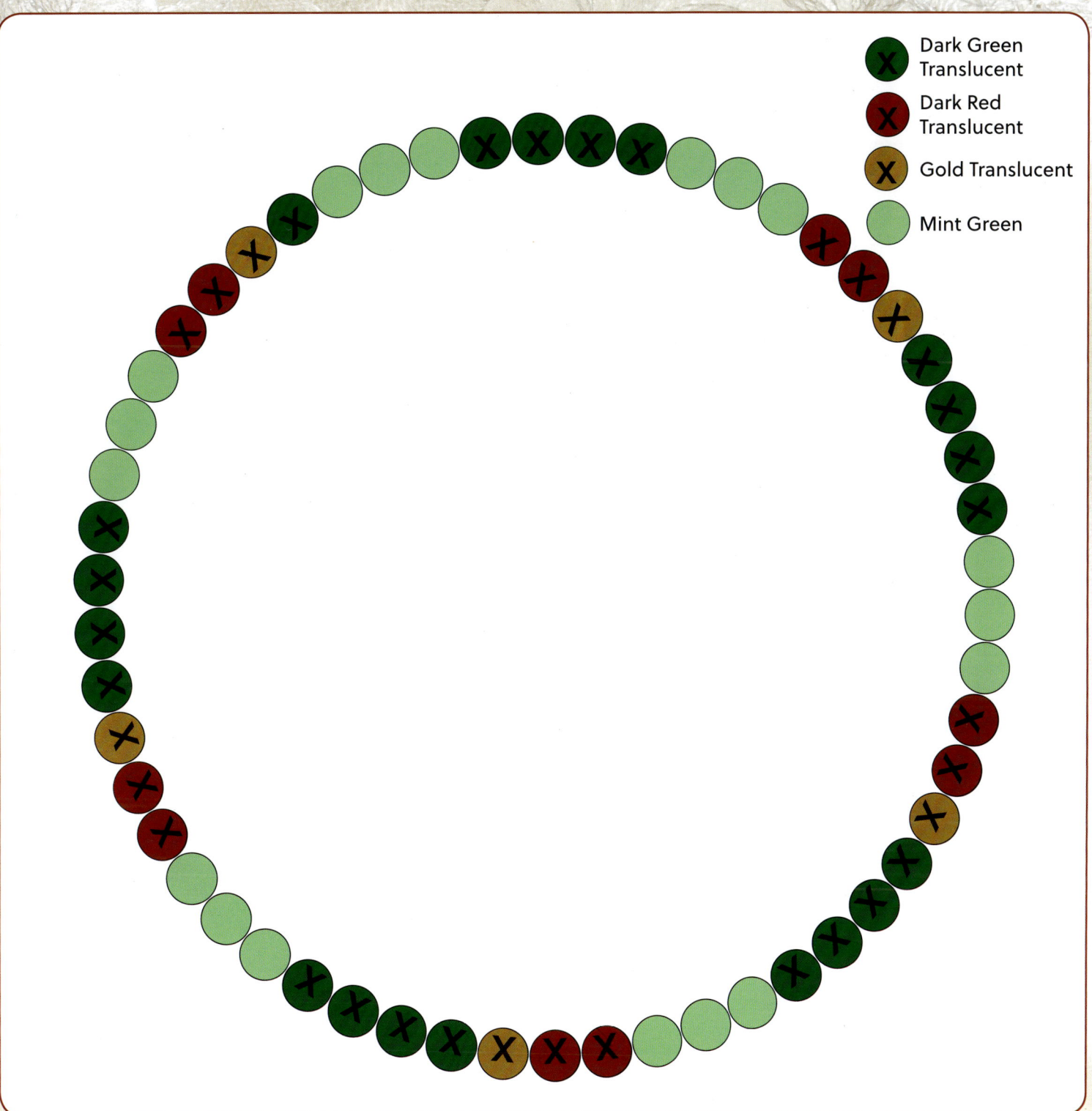

Dark Green Translucent

Dark Red Translucent

Gold Translucent

Mint Green

MIDNIGHTS
Era

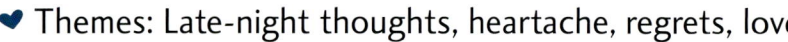

- ❤ Release Date: October 21, 2022

- ❤ Years: 2022–24

- ❤ Popular Songs: "Anti-Hero," "Snow on the Beach," "Midnight Rain," "You're on Your Own, Kid"

- ❤ Themes: Late-night thoughts, heartache, regrets, love

- ❤ Symbols: Lighters, clocks, moon

- ❤ Summary: Taylor's tenth album, *Midnights*, shared her late-night thoughts and feelings with fans. She expressed her reflections through the album. The *Midnights* aesthetic consisted of dark blues, stars, and clocks.

Midnights depicted the human experience
of ruminating late into the night.

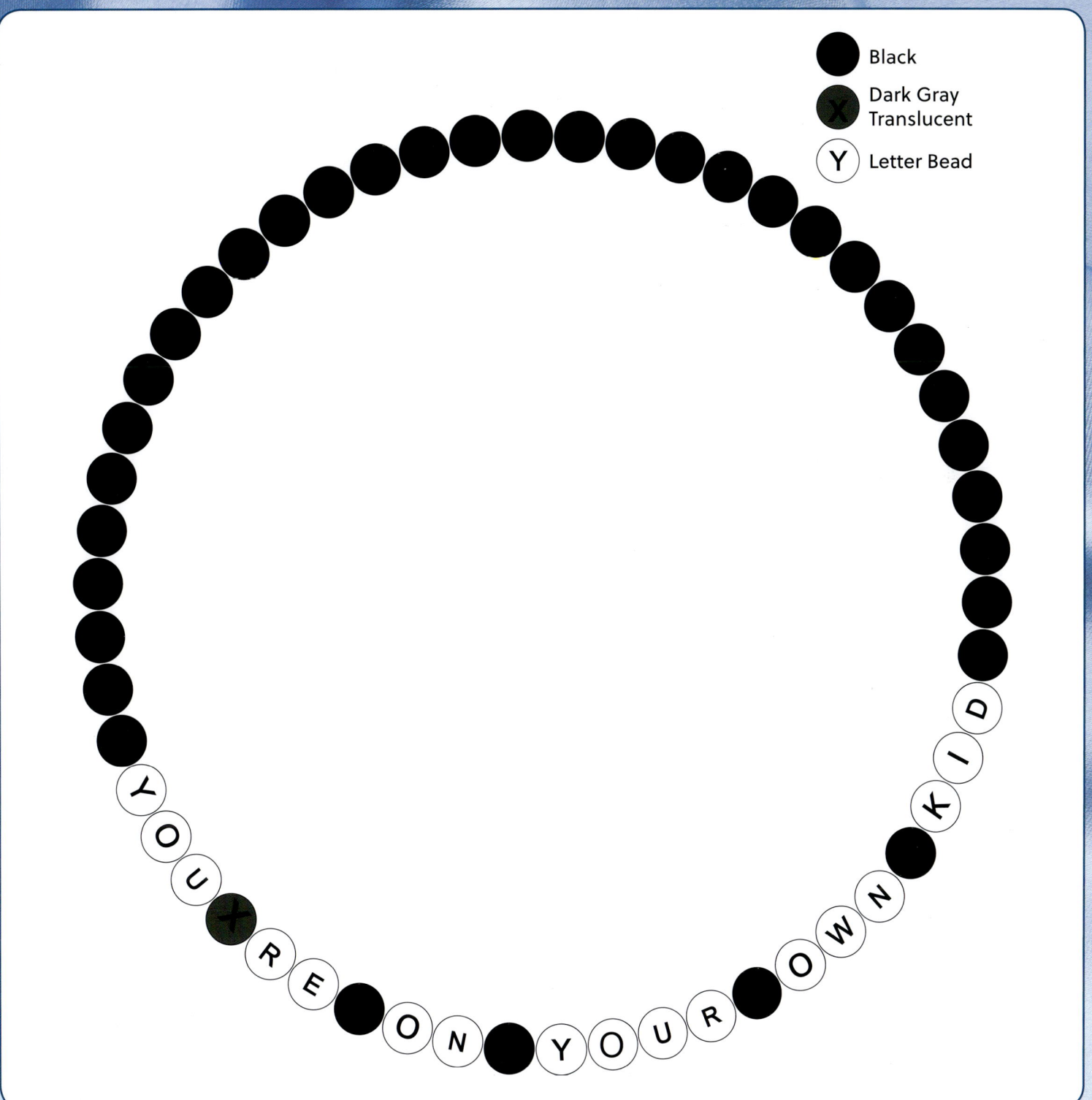

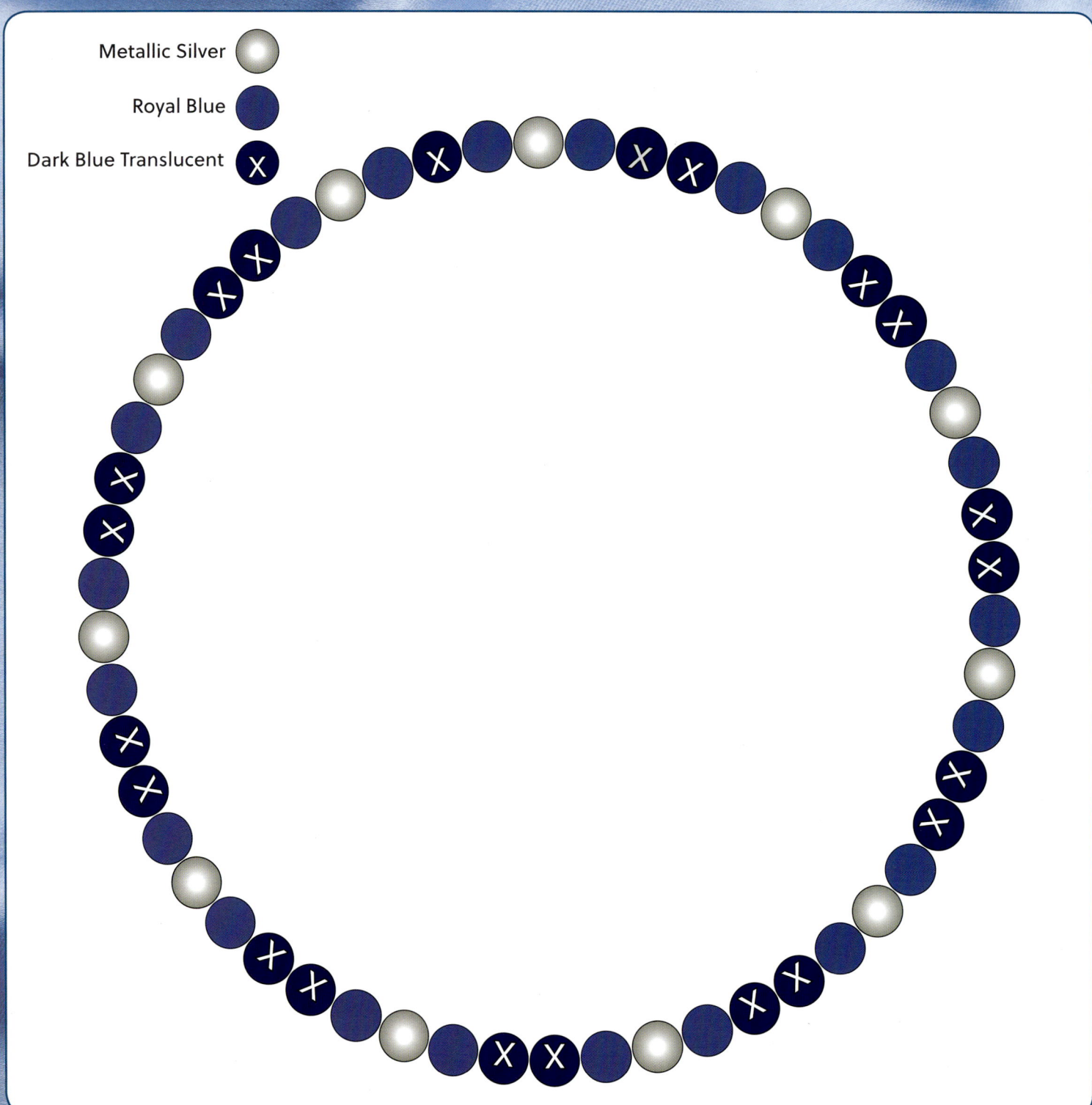

Metallic Silver

Royal Blue

Dark Blue Translucent

Dark Blue Translucent

Gray Translucent

THE TORTURED POETS DEPARTMENT™
Era

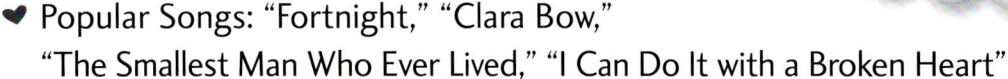

❤ Release Date: April 19, 2024

❤ Years: 2024–

❤ Popular Songs: "Fortnight," "Clara Bow," "The Smallest Man Who Ever Lived," "I Can Do It with a Broken Heart"

❤ Themes: Heartbreak, acceptance, loss, innocent love

❤ Symbols: Black and white, drums, tattoos

❤ Summary: Taylor's eleventh album, *The Tortured Poets Department*™ was the complete opposite of the *Lover*™ era. Instead of bright pastel pinks and blues, Taylor leaned into dull black-and-white aesthetics. The loss of love, heartbreak, and pain were expressed in powerful ballads, such as "The Smallest Man Who Ever Lived."

The Tortured Poets Department™ tackled relatable themes
like gut-wrenching heartbreak, loss of love,
and finding an innocent love.

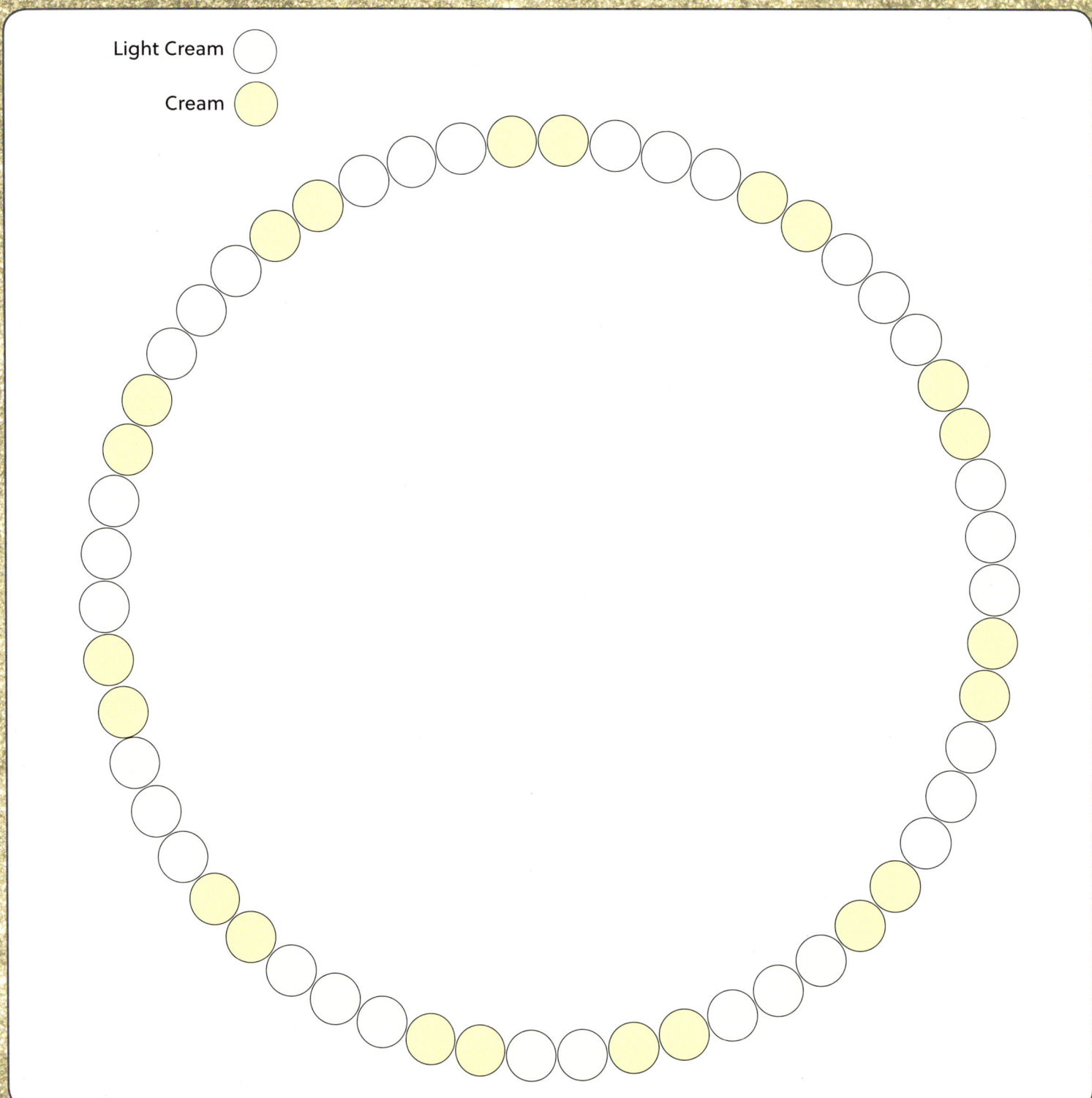

Light Cream

Cream

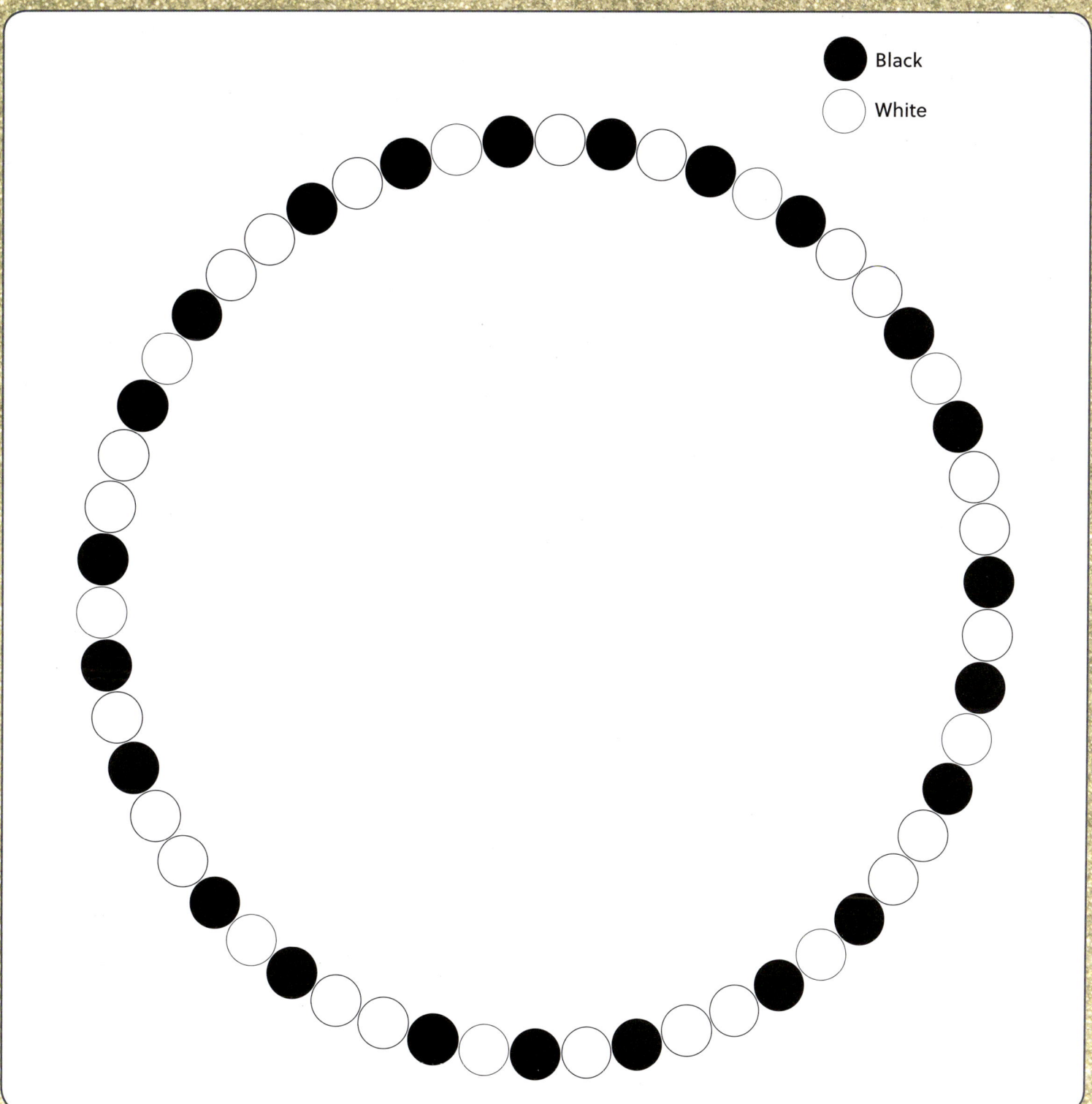

Black
White